Praise for Debra Haffner's books

BEYOND THE BIG TALK
A Parent's Guide to Raising Sexually Healthy Teens

"Writing in an engaging style, Haffner addresses the individual topics families face at different points in adolescence. This highly recommended resource is sure to be welcomed by parents of teenagers—and future teenagers—everywhere."
—*Voice of Youth Advocates*

"Credible and reassuring, Haffner carefully articulates what the range of values might be on a particular issue, but makes it clear that it is up to parents to convey their own values to their children." —*Family Life Matters,* Rutgers University

"I recommend that parents read this book and Haffner's previous one, too. Together they do an excellent job of dealing with what is probably one of the most difficult challenges we will face as parents." —*Chicago Parent* magazine

"Based on years of experience, Debra Haffner provides sound advice to parents on how to talk to their children on sensitive subjects. The book is a must read for every parent."
—Michael H. Merson, M.D., Dean of Public Health, Chairman, Department of Epidemiology and Public Health, Yale University School of Medicine

"Terrific....This wonderful handbook offers advice in a conversational tone [and] opens up a world of opportunities for connection and collaboration." —Harriet Selverstone, President of the American Association of School Librarians

beyond the
BIG TALK

A Parent's Guide to Raising
Sexually Healthy Teens—
From Middle School to High School and Beyond

Revised and Updated Edition

DEBRA W. HAFFNER

NEWMARKET PRESS
New York

*To my parents, Harriet Haffner Hetherington and
Saul Haffner, for their friendship, support, and love—and
for teaching me throughout my childhood and adolescence
to celebrate the gift of my sexuality.*

This book is published in the United States and in Canada.

Revised and Updated Edition

10 9 8 7 6 5 4 3 2 1

Library of Congress Cataloging-in-Publication Data
    Haffner, Debra W.
    Beyond the big talk : Every parent's guide to raising sexually healthy teens—from middle school to high school and beyond / by Debra W. Haffner.—1st ed.
        p. cm.
    1. Sex instruction for teenagers. 2. Parent and teenager. I. Title.
    HQ57.H34   2001   2001030483
    649'65--dc21   CIP

ISBN 978-1-55704-811-0 (paperback)

Quantity Purchases
Companies, professional groups, clubs, and other organizations may qualify for special terms when ordering quantities of this title. For information, write Special Sales Department, Newmarket Press, 18 East 48th Street, New York, NY 10017; call (212) 832-3575; fax (212) 832-3629; or e-mail info@newmarketpress.com.

www.newmarketpress.com

Based on a design by Timothy Shaner

Table of Contents

Contents

Acknowledgments

Writing a new book is a little like pregnancy and childbirth. To the outside world, it may seem as if only the woman is pregnant. But, if we are lucky, we are supported through our pregnancies by a much larger community as we prepare for the birth of a new child.

This book had many midwives and supporters. I am grateful to the Sexuality Information and Education Council of the United States for their permission to adapt sections of a monograph I edited for them, "Facing Facts: Sexual Health for America's Adolescents."

Amy Levine once again provided impeccable research assistance. She was willing to track down arcane facts and make countless trips to libraries for the articles I needed, and was eager to offer suggestions on issues to cover.

My family provided loving support as I worked on this book. Ralph, Alyssa, and Gregory encourage my desire to write and allow me time to do so. My children continue to be my inspiration, my center, and my daily teachers about how to be a better parent. I especially thank Alyssa for being the type of teenage child that every parent wants and for her willingness to have parts of her adolescence shared with my readers.

We are lucky to live within minutes of our extended family, who provide ongoing support and encouragement. My parents, Saul Haffner and Harriet Haffner Hetherington, have always been my biggest supporters and fans. Their spouses, Barbara Jay and Nelson Hetherington, have become my stepparents but more importantly my friends. My sister Jodi Wallace is my confidant, sounding board, and parenting support. My sister-in-law Pat Grande offers wise counsel, an ear to lean on, and the most fabulous bed and breakfast, Grandview in Westerly, Rhode Island, for writing and reflection.

My family of support is much larger than my blood relatives, though. My women's group—Jodi, Tess, Barbara, Barbara, and Rossella—have cheered me on, helped me understand myself, and shared their parenting stories with me. More importantly, we share our lives together.

I have been working for more than twenty-five years in fields related to sexuality and adolescent health. My work has been deeply influenced by many of my colleagues in adolescent health care and sexuality: Peggy Brick, Adele Hoffman, Hillary Millar, Vince Hutchins, Bob Johnson, Bob Blum, Michael Resnick, Lynn Bearinger, Bill Yarber, Sol Gordon, Michael Carrera, Bill Stayton, James Maddox, Eli Coleman, Art Elster, Judith Senderowitz, Karen Hein, Douglas Kirby, and Beth Winship have all influenced my thinking and my understanding of adolescent sexuality, and all have encouraged my work over the years in this area.

Many people have shared their stories with me, both about their own adolescence and their experiences as teens and parents. Warm "thank you"s to Bill Finger, Barbara Huberman, Karen (Kitten) Gross, Ann Thompson Cook, Barbara Levi-Berliner, John Reiss, Pepper Schwartz, Brent Miller, Ledell and Don Mulvaney, Edie Moore, Emily Wallace, Dan Fanneli, Francesca Fanneli, J.D. Lalonde, Marcella Sosa, Richard Del Bello, Eliza Chard, Frank Fanneli, Steve Milender, and Kate Hanley. This is a better book because of their insights.

Acknowledgments

Several of my colleagues and dear friends generously read drafts of parts of this book and offered their comments and suggestions. Dr. Linda Bearinger, Dr. Walter Bockting, Dr. Douglas Kirby, Dr. Brent C. Miller, Monica Rodriguez, Dr. Bob Selverstone, and Dr. Pepper Schwartz offered comments, suggestions, and changes. Their contributions helped make this a better book; the errors of course are all mine. I am grateful to the people at Newmarket Press who believe in the need to educate parents; especially Esther Margolis for wanting to turn my first book into a series and Harry Burton for tirelessly helping to get the word out.

I was very lucky early in my career to have mentors who recognized something in me and believed in my capabilities long before I did. Each of them took a chance on an eager, but inexperienced young woman in her twenties. I am pleased to finally have a formal opportunity to acknowledge my debt to Peter Cott, who first promoted me at the Population Institute; Dr. John Marshall, who made me the director of a national adolescent health initiative while I was at the U.S. Public Health Service; and Mary Janney, who generously trained me to be a spokesperson at Planned Parenthood of Metropolitan Washington, D.C.

This book is dedicated to my parents, Harriet Haffner Hetherington and Saul Haffner. It is at their dinner table that I learned that sexuality was a gift, and something that could be talked about and shared. They encouraged my questions, and they laid the foundation for me to be a sexually healthy adult. I was lucky to have them as my parents; today, I am lucky to have them as my friends.

Introduction to the Revised Edition

It's been nearly eight years since I wrote *Beyond the Big Talk*. It's hard to imagine that pre–September 11th, 2001, world. It was a world before we knew about terrorist threat levels, the Iraq war, and Al-Qaeda.

But, on a less serious level, it was also a world without Facebook and MySpace, *American Idol*, and Paris Hilton. The good news for parents is that teenagers in 2008 are actually more sexually responsible than teenagers five or even fifteen years ago; they are more likely to delay sexual intercourse and more likely to use contraception and condoms when they do become sexually involved. Teenage birth rates were at their lowest level in sixty-five years until they rose ever so slightly in 2006. Yes, you read that right: sixty-five years.

But we also face new challenges in raising our teenage children. I didn't even mention cell phones, iPods, and text-messaging in the first edition of this book. Social networking sites did not exist; today, most teenagers over the age of fourteen have their own Web pages. Three-quarters of teens have Internet access in their homes, up from just slightly more than half when this book was first written.

The sheer volume of sexual content that teens are exposed to has also grown dramatically in this period. On nightly television, sexual content has grown from an average of three sex scenes per hour to five. One in three teens has been exposed unwittingly to sexual content on the Internet, up from one in four just a few years ago.

My own perspectives on parenting have changed as well. My

daughter, Alyssa, who wrote the foreword to this book when she was sixteen, has now graduated from college, moved into her first apartment, and is employed in the reproductive health field. My son, Greg, is now in high school. I've learned directly about parenting a late adolescent on her way to adulthood and a teenage boy. I've also had the privilege of speaking to hundreds of parent groups around the country since this book was first published.

I've updated this volume to include the latest information and insights about adolescent sexuality. I've also written a new book, *What Every 21st-Century Parent Needs to Know: Facing Today's Challenges with Wisdom and Heart,* which goes into more depth about a wide range of parenting issues today.

What has not changed since the first edition is parents' desire to do a better job than their parents did when it comes to educating their children and teenagers about sexuality. And today's children want and expect their parents to be accessible, honest, and forthcoming about sexuality issues. They want us to provide them with information, guidance, and, most important, our time and our love. Talk with them about your values, stay involved, and love your teens extravagantly. Let them know you are always there for them. Help them celebrate their developing sexuality with awareness, delight, responsibility, and caution—in ways that are developmentally appropriate. Reach out for help when you need it; remember to tell them you love them. These years go by very quickly.

Foreword

by Alyssa Haffner Tartaglione, age 16

Whenever I am in situations learning about sex with my peers, I realize how differently I have been brought up. As a toddler, my mother taught me the correct names for the parts of the body and not to use the incorrect names. When shopping with my mom, she asks me what message I am trying to portray in my clothing style. I am never allowed to go to parties without one of my parents talking to the parent of the house where the party is. And for Hanukkah this year I received a copy of *Our Bodies, Ourselves*—a sentimental coming-of-age moment in my mother's eyes. Ever since I was little, my mother has been there to inform me and answer my questions regarding sexuality. Most teenagers I know do not have this type of open communication with their parents on this topic.

But, it's not always easy being the daughter of a sexuality educator. I am often embarrassed by it. My mom will appear in the latest teen magazine in an article, or she will want to talk to my friends about sex. There is not a television show, movie, or story in the news about sex that goes by without her bringing up a conversation about it. My life is an ongoing teachable moment. It sometimes feels like my mom always wants to talk about sex with me.

Nevertheless, it is good to know that I can talk to my mom about anything. Most of my friends don't feel comfortable enough to talk to their parents at all about sexuality. The majority of them were given a book when they turned 12. That was it.

It seems that most parents worry about their teens drinking, doing drugs, dating, going to parties, and most of all, whether we are having sex or not. It doesn't seem like they trust us.

Now, it's true...some of my peers don't make the best decisions. Some of them are rebelling against parents who are too strict...and some of them have parents who just don't seem to care what their child is doing. Many parents have no clue about what it's like to be a teen today. If being a parent of a teen is hard, being a teenager is even harder. A lot of teenagers feel totally stressed—about doing well in school, fitting in, being popular, being attractive, succeeding in sports, and managing it all.

Teenagers do want a good relationship with their parents. And most teens will make good decisions, if you help them. We want to be able to communicate openly in our homes. Most of the teens I know make the right choices and resist peer pressure.

Don't wait for your teen to say, "I want to talk to you about sex today." It's not going to happen. And for sure, don't wait until you find condoms in your kid's room. You will probably have to initiate the discussions. It may be difficult at first, but most teens will talk to their parents if we think you are comfortable talking to us.

That's where this book comes in. I've had firsthand experience with my mom's parenting. I think I'm probably the most qualified person to judge whether or not talking with your children and teens about sexuality can positively affect their lives. I know for sure that it's not true that talking about sex with your teens will encourage sexual behaviors. Talking with your teens will help them make good decisions now and later on in life.

So, here is the bottom line. We want to be able to communicate openly and comfortably with our parents. We want to know our parents are here to help us. Most of all we want to be respected and trusted. Talking with your teens will create this kind of relationship. This book can help you!

Chapter 1
The Basics

$\mathbf{M}$y daughter Alyssa is entering her junior year at high school this fall. I am excited for her as she enters this new phase of adolescence. I am awed as I watch her develop into a young woman. I find myself being caught off guard sometimes when she emerges from upstairs looking very much like a beautiful woman and not at all like our little girl.

And, like most parents of teens, I am more than a little scared. Will she continue to make friends easily? What will it be like when she falls in love for the first time, and what will it be like when someone breaks her heart? How will she handle peer pressure? And are we really prepared to deal with her developing sexuality?

It's not easy being a parent of a teenager today. To be candid, I have found parenting an adolescent to be a humbling experience.

I had always thought I would be a terrific parent of an adolescent child. After all, I have worked with teens for more than two decades. The teenagers in my classes and groups love me. I love their energy, their commitment, and their willingness to challenge adults.

I pride myself on being an adult who understands teens. I know the somewhat predictable stages of adolescent development. I have had years of experience helping teens deal with peer pressure...sexual feelings...the need to begin to be independent from their parents.

And then my daughter Alyssa entered middle school, and theory met practice. She summed it up one day when she was 12, at the end of yet another disagreement. She looked at me derisively and said, "And you're supposed to be an expert in my age group!"

Now, I *am* an expert in her age group. I have worked with adolescents for more than twenty-five years. I have counseled teens at clinics, and I have offered workshops and classes at schools, community agencies, and my church. I have developed programs and materials for teens. I even created and coordinated the activities of the National Commission on Adolescent Sexual Health.

It is true that these experiences will help me be a better parent to Alyssa and our son Gregory as they go through their teen years. It does help to know the developmental stages that your child is likely to go through. It helps to think through the values that you want to communicate about sexuality to your teenagers. It helps to have some ideas about how to get and keep a discussion going with a noncommunicative 16 year old.

But parenting an adolescent is challenging, even for the experts. Each year at the Society for Adolescent Medicine annual meeting, a group of adolescent medicine doctors, psychologists, and nurses meet to discuss what it is like to deal with their own adolescent children. They are experts in other people's teen children; it is their own who are tough to deal with. And helping your child develop a sense of his or her sexual identity is one of the most challenging parts of parenting.

I can hear some of my readers taking a deep breath here. What sexual identity? Who said anything about wanting my child to develop a sexual identity? And what is the author *really* talking about?

Psychologists tell us that forming a sexual identity is a key developmental task of adolescence. What do they mean? First, during adolescence, children mature biologically into adults, developing the capacity to bear children themselves. Second, it is during these years that they experience their first adultlike erotic feelings, and almost all teens will begin to experiment with some sexual behaviors, alone and/or with a partner. Third, they develop a stronger sense of who they are as a man or a woman (this is known as gender identity) and a stronger sense of their own sexual orientation (whether they are homosexual, heterosexual, or bisexual).

All of these changes can be difficult for parents. It is hard to see your "baby" starting to become a sexual person. It is more than a little daunting to realize that your 16-year-old daughter or son has the body of a sexually mature adult. It even can make you feel jealous as you watch your teen's sexuality blossom and contrast it with your own midlife sexual changes.

It can also be scary. The facts about adolescent sexual behavior today can be frightening. Indeed, for a parent of a teenager, they can be downright terrifying.

Consider these facts:

- Almost half of teens in high schools have had sexual intercourse.
- The average teenage girl has her first experience with sexual intercourse in her senior year of high school; the

average teenage boy begins having intercourse during his junior year.

- More than four in ten teenage women will be pregnant by their twentieth birthday.
- More than one in four teens who have sexual intercourse will become infected with a sexually transmitted disease during their teen years.
- The fastest growing group of people who are infected with HIV, the virus that causes AIDS, are young people aged 15 to 24.

These facts do not just happen to other people's children. These are not just statistics; each number represents a real live teen and his or her family faced with these difficult life-changing issues. More than nine in ten American teenagers experiment with sexual behaviors. In other words, unless you have a teenage child who is totally asocial, the chances are that while they are in high school they will be exploring their sexuality with another person. Remember that sexuality is not the same thing as sexual intercourse: hand holding and kissing can be intense sexual behaviors for a 15 year old. (Even those asocial teens are probably exploring their sexuality on their own through masturbation, books, magazines, and the Internet.) Teenage pregnancies and sexually transmitted diseases affect teens of all races, all socioeconomic groups, urban teens, rural teens, and teens who live in every state in the country.

Okay, so stop and take a deep breath. When I am speaking with groups of parents of adolescents and share these statistics with them, their faces often become pale. I have even noticed some parents who put their heads in their hands! Parents are understandably shaken when they hear these facts for the first time. Please take another deep breath.

Because I want you to know that this book is about the *good news*. What if I told you that your actions and your involvement in your teen's life could make a difference? I promise you that if you follow the advice in this book, you can *increase the chances* that your teenager will not become involved in sexual behaviors that they are not ready to handle. Of course, I cannot promise you that this will work for all teens or that your child will not have sexual intercourse during their teenage years. If you have made it as far in parenting to having an adolescent, you know that not every strategy works for all children and that some children are more difficult to raise than others are. As you will see throughout this book, I believe in obtaining outside counseling and assistance for troubled teens.

But, for the majority of teenagers, good parenting can make the difference. In a study of more than twelve thousand teenagers from around the country, researchers at the University of North Carolina and the University of Minnesota found that parental guidance matters. When teens feel connected to their parents, the chances that they will be involved in risk behaviors, from drinking to drugs to violence to unprotected sexual intercourse, all go down. Physically being with your children at key times of the day—when they wake up, after school, at dinner, and at bedtime—makes a difference, but not as big a difference as whether your teenage children feel you love them and care for them. They discovered that in homes where parents have given their teen children clear messages that indicate that they disapprove of teens having intercourse, these teens are more likely to delay becoming involved in sexual intercourse. Other studies have indicated that in homes where parents and teens talk about sexuality, the teen is more likely to wait to have intercourse and more likely to use contraception and condoms when he or she does become sexually experienced.

Sexually Healthy Families

In my book *From Diapers to Dating: A Parent's Guide to Raising Sexually Healthy Children*, I introduced the idea of sexually healthy families. Sexually healthy families raise sexually healthy children and adolescents who grow up to become sexually healthy adults.

Now, before you get upset, let me explain that "sexuality" is different than sex or sexual behaviors. I am not talking about sexual behaviors when I talk about sexually healthy families. Sexuality is about who we are as men and women, and not about what we do with a part of our bodies. Sexuality encompasses an individual's sexual knowledge, beliefs, attitudes, values, and behaviors. Your sexuality is not defined just by your body and your feelings. It is also shaped by your cultural background, your family history, your education, your experiences, and your religion. We are sexual beings from birth to death.

So what do I mean when I talk about a sexually healthy adolescent? A sexually healthy adolescent is not defined by the behaviors he or she abstains from or the behaviors he or she engages in. There are teen virgins who are not sexually healthy and sexually experienced teens who may be. And vice versa. Our sexuality is about much more than our reproductive organs or what we do with our genitals. According to the National Commission on Adolescent Sexual Health, sexually healthy adolescents appreciate their bodies, take responsibility for their own behaviors, communicate effectively within their families, communicate effectively with both genders in appropriate and respectful ways, and express love and intimacy in a manner that is appropriate for their age.

Sexually healthy adolescents do not just happen. They have parents who consider educating their teens about sexuality an important responsibility, and these parents create homes where sexuality is discussed naturally and easily. Sexually healthy teenagers know that they can always come to their parents for assistance and that they are truly loved.

And many parents let our teens down in this important area. In a recent study by the Kaiser Family Foundation, almost four in ten parents said that they had not talked to their teenage children about relationship issues and about becoming sexuality active. Fewer than half had talked to their children about how to prevent pregnancies and sexually transmitted diseases if they did become sexually active. (But these parents were doing better than their parents had done: Fewer than two in ten remembered talking with their own parents about sexually transmitted diseases or contraception.)

Recently, my daughter Alyssa was on a panel at a retreat with other teenagers talking about sexuality and teens. At the end of it, she said to me, "Mom, I realize I'm being raised really differently than most kids." When I asked her what that meant, she said, "Most kids have never talked to their parents about sexuality; all their parents did was give them a book when they turned 12." In fact, this "book syndrome" seems to be quite common. Many parents have told me that they bought their child a book on sexuality or puberty, left it in the preteen's room, and never discussed it again.

Try to take this quiz as honestly as possible:

- Do you respect your teenager?
- Do you trust your teenager?
- Are you knowledgeable about sexuality?
- Do you model sexually healthy attitudes in your own primary intimate relationship?
- Do you talk with your teens regularly about sexuality issues?

- Do you really try to understand your adolescent's point of view?
- Do you set and maintain limits for dating and other activities outside of school?
- Are you actively involved in your teen's life?
- Do you ask questions about his or her friends and romantic partners?
- Do you provide a supportive and safe environment for your children?
- Do you offer to assist your teens in finding reproductive health care?

How many "yes's" can you honestly give yourself? Are there areas that you might want to improve? A "yes" answer tells you that you have one of the characteristics of a sexually healthy parent as defined by the National Commission on Adolescent Sexual Health. In the coming chapters, I will present ideas and scenarios that may be helpful as you parent your adolescent.

There are many different types of families today, and I believe that all types can be sexually healthy for children and teens. Many of you may be your child's biological parents, but many of you may be grandparents, aunts and uncles, foster parents, or adoptive parents. In this book, I have tried to be inclusive of all kinds of parenting arrangements. There are special issues that affect single parents, parents who are divorced, and parents who are gay and lesbian, and I will include some special sections in coming chapters about these issues. For the most part though, the advice applies to all types of families and parents who want help on how to raise teens who affirm their sexuality in responsible and healthy ways.

"Good Kids"

We all know teenagers who come from good homes with good parents who still get in trouble in school, with drinking and driving, and with sex. We also know teenagers who apparently succeed despite their troubled family backgrounds or situations.

Americans are surprisingly down on teenagers. In a study by the nonprofit group Public Agenda, most Americans said they are disappointed with "kids these days," and almost three-quarters used negative words to describe the average teenager, such as rude, irresponsible, and wild. Only one in six used positive words to describe teenagers. Of course, there is nothing new about youth upsetting their elders. More than two thousand years ago, Socrates described youth this way: "They are also mannerless and fail to rise when their elders enter the room. They chatter before company, gobble up dainties at the table, cross their legs, and tyrannize over their teachers."

Fortunately, most teenagers feel pretty good about themselves. Almost three-quarters of teens say, "I can always trust my parents to be there for me when I need them." Two-thirds say, "Faith in God is an important part of my life," and almost two-thirds say, "I can always trust my friends to be there for me when I need them." Half say, "I am usually happy." I think that a big part of our job as parents is to help strengthen our teens and help them flourish.

There has been a lot of research in the past several years about what psychologists call vulnerability and resilience. In other words, what makes "good kids" good? What makes some kids flourish? What makes some kids more likely to be involved with violence, substance abuse, and teenage pregnancy? And how can parents help?

Healthy teens are said to have four C's: Competence,

Connection, Character, and Confidence. Competence has to do with the teen's ability to do well at school, socially, and at work. Connection is about whether the teen has caring relationships with peers, parents, family, and other adults in the community. Character refers to qualities such as honesty, community service, responsible decision-making, and integrity. Confidence is when a young person has hope, self-esteem, and goals for his or her future.

Families and schools are probably the biggest influence on how young people will manage their adolescence. An organization called the Search Institute in Minnesota has actually identified forty characteristics of communities and families that help young people to grow up to be healthy, caring, and responsible.

Young people are more likely to do well if they come from families that provide high levels of support and love, and where the teens communicate and seek advice and counsel from their parents. The problem is that most parents fail their children in this important area. Too many parents develop what I'm going to call the "Missing Parent Syndrome" when their children become adolescents. I recently met a 13-year-old girl with a mother who sends her e-mails twice a day from her home office with a list of things to do, instead of sitting down and talking with her. Part of the "Missing Parent Syndrome" happens because today's dual-career couple or single parents are working many more hours. According to the Institute of Medicine, as much as 40 percent of young adolescents' time is unstructured, unsupervised, and unproductive.

But it is not just a problem of having less physical time together. Many parents of teens begin to remove themselves from their children's lives. They stop setting limits for their teenage child's behavior. They stop asking questions about where their teen children are going after school or on the weekends. They tell me, "I've tried everything and I don't know what to do. I give up."

They leave their teenagers alone in the house for long periods of time without supervision, or even go away on the weekends and leave their teens in charge of the house. They feel that their teens are too old to arrange for supervision or camp or to take with them on vacation. Do you remember the movie *Risky Business?* The Tom Cruise character has a huge party when his parents leave him alone for the weekend and even becomes involved with a prostitute. Well, this doesn't just happen in the movies. In our town, the police tell me that they break up teen parties each year where there are no parents at home. In fact, one group of teens told me that every party they go to is broken up by police!

The first and primary lesson of this book is *stay involved.* One of the saddest things I ever read was an interview with the dad of one of the teen boys who murdered the other children at Columbine High School. The father was reported to say, "But I thought I had finished parenting."

You are not finished. In fact, raising an adolescent is one of the most important and challenging parts of parenting. You have probably heard the adage, "Little children, little problems. Big children, big problems." Helping your teen successfully navigate his or her sexuality is one of the biggest challenges of raising an adolescent. According to the Institute of Medicine, if parents provide guidance, discipline, and close supervision, their teen children are less likely to engage in intercourse, drugs, and antisocial behaviors.

But it is more than parents that determine which teens do well. "Good kids" also have caring neighbors and a caring, encouraging school environment. The Search Institute found that "good kids" have at least three other adults in their lives besides their parents who care about them. One study found that teens who said they have adult mentors were less likely to have intercourse. Stop and think for a moment: How many significant adults are in your teen's life? If your teen felt he couldn't come to you with a problem, are there are other adults he could go to comfortably? Does your daughter have other adults in her life that she trusts and with whom she relates well?

They also found that "good kids" are actively involved in school, community, and religious institutions. Indeed, the research indicates that these young people are involved in more than seventeen hours a week of activities in addition to the time they spend at school.

Thinking about your teenage child, how many hours a week does he or she:

- Spend in lessons or practice music, theater, or other arts?
- Spend in youth programs, such as sports, clubs, or organizations at school or in the community?
- Spend in activities at a church, synagogue, or mosque?
- Read for pleasure?
- Do homework?
- Hang out with friends "with nothing special to do"?

Here is how the teens in the Search Institute's study that are "healthy, caring, and responsible" spend time each week:

- Three hours in creative activities
- Three hours in youth programs
- One or more hours at a religious institution
- Doing at least one hour of homework a night
- Reading for pleasure three or more hours a week

And maybe, most importantly, they spend time at home with their families. These "good kids" hang out with their friends with "nothing special to do" two or fewer nights per week. How does *your* teenager spend his or her time? Do you know? And if your teen doesn't seem to be doing any of these activities, how can you encourage him or her to do so? It's unreasonable to expect that your couch-potato or computer-fixated teen will all of a sudden add seventeen hours of activities to their life each week; start by asking them to do one!

"Good kids" also hang around with other "good kids." As I will repeat in several of the upcoming chapters, knowing your teen's friends is imperative. Adolescents spend about twice as much time with their friends as their parents. In general, teens choose friends who share their values; research tells us that most teens have two to four "best friends" who are pretty much like themselves. Teens who don't drink or smoke or have sex are unlikely to choose friends who do. As adults, we are often concerned that teens will be overwhelmed by "peer pressure." What the research tells us is that peer pressure can be positive as well as negative: The right peer group makes the difference. (I will talk about what to do if you don't like your teen's friends or boyfriend or girlfriend in upcoming chapters.)

The Search Institute also found that teens who do well have a strong positive sense of their own identity. They believe that they have control over the "things that happen to me." They report having a high sense of self-esteem. They report, "My life has a purpose." They are optimistic about their personal future.

Some of my readers are now breathing a sigh of relief: "My teen does most of these things." Some of you are probably feeling a little anxious: "My teenager never seems to get off the computer." Some of you may be feeling that your teen doesn't quite match up to the Search Institute's criteria for a "good kid." Some of you may be worrying that your child is one of the kids that other parents are concerned about. Later on in this book, I will have suggestions for all of you.

The point I want to make here is that parents can influence many of these variables. Of course, parents set the tone for the home environment: You can make sure that you have family dinners at least a few times a week, that you are there as often as you can be at bedtime, and that your children *know* that you love and care for them. Now, I know that none of us are perfect parents, and that many of us have lives that mean that we are at work at dinner time or bedtime, or that we are struggling to just maintain our families' lives. Parenting is tough; think through some easy ways to make sure your child knows that you care. A cell phone call or text message at bedtime or a note on a pillow if you can't be there can help your child know he or she is loved.

You can also encourage your child's involvement in other activities. You can recommend that they do volunteer work in your community. You can encourage their involvement in sports, drama, music, or youth group programs. (Not all children will want to do all of these, nor will they have the natural talent to do some of them at the high school level.) What is important is that they get involved in *something* besides school and home. You can ask them to go to worship services with you. You can encourage them to become friends with other adults: a youth group leader, youth minister, aunt or uncle, Big Brother or Big Sister, or family friends.

You can also encourage them to do well in school. Parents can monitor if homework is being completed and offer assistance if needed. You can attend back-to-school nights and talk with their teachers if problems arise. You can talk to your children about their plans for their future, and if they are academically inclined, help prepare them for college.

You may be asking yourself, "What does this have to do with sex and sexuality?" Well, the research tells us that teens who feel good about themselves, teens who do well in school, and teens who are busy with meaningful activities are less likely to become sexually involved before they are emotionally ready. For example, in a study a few years ago of teenage girls who are athletes, teen athletes were less likely to have had sexual intercourse, less likely to have been pregnant, and, for those who were engaging in sexual intercourse, more likely to have used condoms if they did have sex compared to girls who were not involved in sports. In other studies, involvement in just one after-school club decreased involvement in risk-taking behaviors, reduced the probability of a teen birth, and increased the chances of high school completion.

After having worked with thousands of teens, my hunch is that the most important way to prevent early sexual involvement and teenage pregnancies is for young people to have adults in their lives who care about them and hold them to high standards. In other words, it doesn't matter whether your teen children are in field hockey, Girl Scouts, the band, the chess club, or the church youth group, as long as they are actively involved in something outside of the home with caring, concerned adults who hold them accountable. These feelings of self worth and positive identity are also a crucial foundation for healthy adult intimate relationships.

Adult Amnesia

I am amazed by how often adults act as if they were never teenagers themselves. All of us are ex-adolescents. You once experienced the joys, the frustrations, and the awkwardness of being a teenager. You probably fell in love for the first time when you were a teenager. You probably had your first orgasm when you were a teenager. You probably had your first sexual experiences as a teenager, even if they didn't involve sexual intercourse...even if they did not involve another person!

Before we go any further, I want you to try to remember what it was like to be an adolescent. Perhaps you want to shut your eyes and picture yourself as a 15-year-old. You might want to look through an old scrapbook to find some pictures of yourself as a teenager. Or better yet, see if you can pull out your old high school yearbook.

Now try to remember:

- How did you feel about your body? Did you like the way you looked?
- What type of clothes did you wear? What did your hair and makeup look like?
- How do you think adults felt about your appearance?
- What was it like to hold hands on a date for the first time?
- Where did you go on your first date? What did you do? Who was it with? How did you feel before the date? During? After?
- Who was the first person you kissed? Who was the first person you French kissed? Did you like it? Hate it? Where were you? Did you tell your parents about it? (Probably not, right?)
- Who was your first serious crush? Was it unrequited or did they "like you back"? How did you find out?
- Who was your first love? How did you know that you were in love?
- How did the adults around you react to your being in love? (Did the adults around you even know you were in love?)

- What were your sexual behaviors with the first person you were in love with? How did you decide how far to go sexually? Did you talk to your parents about this? (Again, probably not, right?)
- How did you think about your sexuality when you were fifteen? Did you masturbate? Talk about sexuality with your friends? Wonder what it would be like to have sexual intercourse? Ever fantasize about sex with someone of the same gender? The other gender?

How did it feel to go back and remember these feelings? For some of us, adolescence was a breeze. For others of us, it was undeniably painful, confusing, and lonely. It is the same for teens today.

Teens today probably experience many of the same feelings about their sexuality that you did when you were a teen. Excited. Aroused. Scared. Afraid mom and dad will find out their thoughts...actions...relationships...fantasies.

This is not to say that there have not been any changes. Adolescent sexual behavior has changed dramatically since my own mother was a teenager. My mom was married at eighteen and was pregnant with me at nineteen. She, like most of her friends, experimented with sexual behaviors but did not have intercourse until her wedding night. In the 1950s, petting was the most common teenage sexual experience; adolescents reached physical maturity later and married earlier; and teenage intercourse was uncommon except for the oldest and often engaged or married adolescents.

However, adolescent sexual behaviors have changed far less dramatically than when we were teenagers. Indeed, it was our generation (I'm assuming that if you are a parent of an adolescent you are probably between ages 35 and 55, although some of you may be younger or older) that really changed the norms of teenage sexual behavior. It was the oldest of the baby boomers who proclaimed, "Make love, not war." They radically changed the acceptance of sex on college campuses. And for those of us who are a little younger, it was our generation that made teenage sexual intercourse a statistical norm. Between 1971 and 1979, the percentage of teenagers having sexual intercourse increased by two-thirds. People are often surprised when I tell them that the average age of first intercourse has gone down only one year since 1970! In 1970, the average age for first intercourse for boys was 17, and for girls it was 18. Today, the average age is 17 for girls and 16 for boys. That is a one-year difference, despite all of the hype and media stories about how much sooner teens are becoming sexually involved.

Compared to their grandparents, today's teenagers reach physical maturity earlier and marry later. Records from family Bibles around the time of the American Revolution indicate that girls had their first period, what health care professionals call menarche, around the age of 17. In 1860, the average age of menarche was a little more than 15. Today, the average age is 12, and a new study recently found that a significant number of girls are beginning the changes of puberty as early as the second and third grade. The average age of marriage increased from 20 for girls and 23 for boys in 1950 to 25 for girls and 27 for boys in 2005. More than half of teenagers today begin to have intercourse while they are in high school, and most will have several sexual partners before they get married.

One of the most serious changes today's teens have to face is the HIV/AIDS epidemic. When I was in college in the mid-1970s, I didn't know anyone who worried much about the possibility of getting sexually transmitted diseases. We had a sense that syphilis and gonorrhea were curable, and it was before most people knew about herpes. In contrast, today's teenagers have always understood their sexuality in an environment that includes HIV and AIDS. The first cases of AIDS were diagnosed in 1981; the virus and our understanding of its transmission were discovered in 1985. Teens like my daughter have known about AIDS since they were tiny children, and there is no question that AIDS has affected their sense of themselves as sexual beings.

HIV/AIDS. Pregnancies. Sexually Transmitted Diseases. Early Sexual Initiation. I hope I have convinced you that you have to become actively involved with helping your teen deal with these complex issues. The keys are being actively involved in your teenager's life and knowing how to communicate about these issues.

Communication Tips

I know that some of you are saying to yourself, "All well and good, but my teenager is never at home." During Alyssa's first year at high school, she had band practice three nights a week and all day Saturday. She spent most of her weekends at band competitions; we cheered for the band from the stands, often picking her up back at the school parking lot after midnight. During band season, family dinners were reduced to Sunday and Monday evenings. And for many families with teens, even when the teens are at home, they often answer our simple "What did you do today?" with just as simple an answer, "NOTHING."

And if we are not communicating with them about what happened in school today, even fewer parents are talking to their teens about sexual health issues. In one study of 14- to 17-year-olds, only one in two teens reported talking to their mothers about how to make the decision about when to have intercourse, only four in ten reported talking to them about physical development, and only one in six said that they had talked to their mothers about masturbation. But they talked to their fathers even less: Only one-third recalled a conversation with their father about deciding to have sex, only 15 percent had talked with dad about physical development, and only 8 percent had discussed masturbation with him. Both boys and girls were more likely to talk with their mothers than their fathers about sexual topics; but as one might expect, boys were more likely to talk with their dads than girls were. For example, more than half of teen boys reported that their dads had talked to them about condoms; only 27 percent of girls had had such a discussion.

Here's a quick quiz to see how you are communicating with your teenager about sexuality topics. Place a check in the box next to each topic you've discussed with your teen.

Communication Quiz for Parents
Have you and your teenager talked together about:
- ❑ Dating?
- ❑ Abstaining from sexual intercourse?
- ❑ Contraception?
- ❑ Condoms?
- ❑ Setting sexual limits?
- ❑ Your values about premarital sexual behavior?
- ❑ HIV/AIDS?
- ❑ Love?
- ❑ Marriage?
- ❑ Sexual pleasure? Orgasm?
- ❑ Sexual harassment?
- ❑ Date rape?

❏ Sexual orientation?
❏ Alcohol and drugs and sex?
❏ What to do if he or she is thinking about having sexual intercourse?
❏ What to do if she thinks she might be pregnant or have sexually transmitted diseases?
❏ Your hopes for the future?
❏ Media portrayals of sexuality?
❏ Your religious values about sexuality?
❏ Important qualities in a romantic partner?
❏ The kind of relationship he or she should have before having sex?

Scoring

Give yourself one point for each box you checked.

- 18 to 23 points: Congratulations, you are clearly a parent who is already communicating with your child about sexual issues.
- 11 to 17 points: You have begun talking to your child about important sexual issues. By the end of this book, you will be a pro.
- Fewer than ten points: Don't worry, you have time and you have taken the first steps by beginning to read this book.

It might be interesting to ask your teenager to take this quiz as well, asking them whether they think you have talked with them about each subject. In one study, mothers and teens disagreed about half the time about whether a subject had been discussed, with moms saying it had been talked about much more frequently than their children. For example, in about one-quarter of the mother-child pairs studied, the moms said that they had discussed with their children birth control, HIV/AIDS, physical development, and pressures to have sex—and the teen children said they had *not* talked about these subjects. Sometimes, we only *think* we have been communicating!

Here are some basic guidelines that I have found helpful in my professional and personal life for communicating with teens about sexuality:

Remember that your teenager wants to talk with you about your values. In study after study, teenagers tell researchers that they want to talk with their parents about what is important to them. In a study conducted for the Kaiser Family Foundation and Children Now, more than nine in ten teens said that they were glad to have talked with their parents about alcohol and drugs, violence, AIDS, and sex, and more than nine in ten said their parents had given them good ideas on how to handle these issues in their lives. Only one in five youths say that they do not want to hear about sexuality from their parents. More than one-quarter of teens said that the most important issue for their parents to talk to them about was sexually transmitted diseases and pregnancy prevention; one in five said dating, relationships, and sex; one in five wanted their parents to talk with them about when and how to refuse a sexual encounter.

But first it is important to know which values you want to communicate. Many parents of teenagers have not really taken the time to think through their own opinions and values concerning adolescent sexuality. In each of the coming chapters, I will give you some quiz questions to clarify your values about issues that may be affecting your teenager. There are no right or wrong answers, only the answers that reflect your own family values. As I have talked to parents while I was writing this book, I have been impressed by the wide diversity of values about sexuality that people want to pass on to their children. You and your child's other parent are the only people who can teach your very personal values about sexuality to your teen. If you don't do it, who will?

And sharing your values makes a difference. In a study by the U.S. Centers for Disease Control and Prevention, teenagers who said they had talked to their parents frequently about topics such as birth control, HIV, puberty, and reproduction were more likely to share their parents' values about teenage sexuality than teenagers who had not talked much to their folks. Let them know what you think!

Do not have a "Big Talk" about sexuality with your teenager. One of the biggest myths about parents providing sexuality education to their children is that you can do it in a single talk. Every week at SIECUS, the organization I headed for twelve years, the library gets calls asking about what should be included in the Big Talk. I have even seen books and magazine articles on preparing for the Big Talk.

Did your mother or father ever sit you down for a Big Talk on sexuality when you were a teenager? Some of us even received the talk the night before we were married! The fact is that the Big Talk probably did not work with you, and it is not going to work with your teenager either. The only thing the Big Talk is likely to accomplish is to teach your child that you are both uncomfortable talking with each other about sexuality issues.

Teaching your child about sexuality is like teaching your child about other important value issues. I have never heard anyone suggest that we give our children a single Big Talk about God, religion, or even table manners. It is important that parents do it little by little, looking for what sexuality educators call "teachable moments." Teachable moments are the everyday moments that arise naturally to easily provide your teenager with sexuality information or your values. It may be about a story in the news; it may be your reaction to a television program you are watching together; it may be a song on your teen's new CD. It may be when you or your teenager is getting ready for a date. It may have to do with one of their class assignments for social studies, English, or health class. In each chapter, I will point out some teachable moments that are likely to arise when your teen is at a particular stage of development.

Many parents of teenagers complain to me that their child does not ask them questions about sexuality. If you have been less than open with your children about sexuality up until now, it is unlikely that they are going to come home tonight and at the dinner table say, "I was wondering what you think about masturbation, Dad." Or, "Can you tell me more about how effective condoms are?" Do not wait for your child to ask you questions or show interest before you introduce discussions about sexuality. Look for the teachable moments.

Unlike with smaller children though, you need to develop a subtle tack in identifying these moments as teachable to your child. One 14-year-old son of a good friend of mine said to her, "Mom, can we just *watch* television without you always looking for a teachable moment?" Several years ago, Alyssa and I were having a pretty frank discussion about sexual pleasure. After a few minutes, she left my room and headed for her bedroom. I continued talking. She yelled out to me, "Mom, you're having a teachable moment on your own!" She was right.

You do not have to feel comfortable, and you do not have to have all the answers. Countless parents have told me that they are reluctant to talk about sexuality because they might

feel embarrassed, or because they are afraid they will look fool-
ish when they do not know the answers to questions that might
arise. It is okay; I sometimes feel uncomfortable talking about
sexuality with my children, and I do this for a living! You can
tell your teenager if you are feeling uncomfortable: "Wow, I
guess I'm getting a little embarrassed. It's hard for me to talk
about these issues openly. My parents never really talked to me
much about sex. But, I think it is so important, that I want us
to be able to talk about this stuff."

And, what if they stump you with a question? That's okay,
too. None of us know everything about sexuality, not even me.
A few years ago I was teaching a group of middle school students at my church, and we had an "anonymous question box"
where they could leave us questions that they wanted to ask
confidentially. Every week, one of them managed to stump me
with a question. (Question: How large is the largest penis ever
measured? Answer: Few American men are more than nine
inches long when erect. Most men's penises measure between
five and seven inches erect. Question: Is it true that the King
of England gives out condoms on his birthday? Answer: No, but
the King of Thailand does.)

The point is that you can expect that your child will have
questions that you may not know how to answer. Say so, and
then offer to help your teen find out the information. I do not
believe it is ever appropriate to lie or make up information. It
may even help your teen to know that you don't know everything. (Many teens go through a period where they think their
parents know *nothing*!) In some places in this book, I provide
detailed information about some issues, but I may not have
included everything your child wants to know. Check the
index and the Appendix for sources of information. You can
look at one of the Internet sites listed in the Appendix for

answers to many of their questions; the Go Ask Alice site at Columbia University has hundreds of questions and answers, and even allows you to leave a question for them to research. Of course, more traditional information sources like librarians and school nurses might be able to help as well.

Listen to your teenager's point of view. I have a greeting card on my bulletin board that says, "What people need is a good listening to." This is especially true for teenagers. Teenagers often believe, sometimes rightly so, that adults do not care what they think. Some parents believe that their job is to tell their children what to do, and it is their children's job to follow their commands. This probably did not work particularly well when your child was younger; it definitely will not work now that your child is a teenager. Communication is a two-way process: Listening to your teen's point of view is as important as giving them your point of view. It may not come easily to you; practice saying things like, "Tell me what you think about this." "When your friends talk about _____, what are they saying?" "I'd like to know what you are thinking."

There are many different styles of parenting, but some are going to be more effective with most teenagers. Teenagers want parents who are involved, who set limits, but do so with an open mind and with affection. According to the Institute of Medicine and the National Research Council, the research shows that teens need loving, warm, yet firm and consistent parenting. Authoritarian parents—parents who lay down the law but don't listen to their teen's point of view—often have the most rebellious teenage children. They definitely have the most conflicts with their teen children. In fact, in one study I read several years ago, teenage boys with mothers who were fundamentalist Protestants were more likely to have had sexual intercourse than teens with more liberal parents, and teenage girls with mothers with more liberal attitudes toward premarital sex were actually less likely than other teens to have had intercourse. One can imagine that the boys in the fundamentalist Protestant homes were more likely to be rebelling, and the girls in the liberal homes needed to prove themselves less.

On the other hand, teenagers don't want their parents to just be their friends. Overly permissive parenting is also likely to lead your teenager into risk taking. These parents may listen to their teens, but they are afraid to set limits for their teen's behavior. Their children may think their parents are "cool," but they are also more likely to experiment with alcohol, drugs, and sexual behaviors. Some psychologists have labeled this "indulgent parenting" and warn parents to avoid the "Happiness Trap." Parents who want their children to never be angry with them may be loving and warm, but they also fail to help their child set limits. I can't begin to count the number of times I have said to Alyssa, "It's okay if you don't like me very much right now because of the limit I've set. My job right now is to keep you safe; we'll be friends when you are an adult."

Worst of all are the parents who are "rejecting or neglecting" or just absent. These parents neither hold their teens to standards of behaviors nor talk to them, creating in the words of Doris Blazer, a parenting educator from Furman University, "an inconsistent patchwork of limits and love."

The best kind of parent for a teenager is likely to be a blend of styles. Psychologists label these parents as "authoritative," or what I prefer to name "affirming." Think about Bill Cosby's parenting on *The Cosby Show*. Affirming parents set limits for their teen's behavior, but they are also willing to listen and to negotiate. They explain their rules, but they are also responsive to their teen's changing developmental needs. They hold their children accountable for their actions, teach them that their behaviors have consequences, but they never withdraw affection from their children. They are affectionate, pay close attention to their children, and treat them more like equals. Children of affirming parents do better in school, are more popular with other teens, have a higher sense of self-esteem and competence, and engage in fewer risk-taking behaviors.

Let your teen know that you expect them to make mistakes and that you will love them no matter what. Too many of our teenagers think they have to be "perfect" for their parents. Many teenagers today report that stress is their number-one concern. They feel pressure to do well in school, participate in lots of activities, and get into the right college. They worry about disappointing their parents and/or letting them down.

Think back for a minute to your own teenage years. Did you take any risks that would have shocked your parents? Almost every adult I know can remember doing some things as an adolescent that they would be upset to find out that their own teenager was doing. Now, for some of us, this means recalling our own adolescent sexual experiences or alcohol and drug use. I was a proverbial "good girl" in high school, and I still took some unbelievable risks. I remember going drag racing on a stretch of an interstate with a boy in a souped-up car with no muffler. I still cannot drink German wine because of the night I drank too much of it on a date with a college student at age 17.

I can almost guarantee that your teenager will take risks that you wish they wouldn't, and that they will make mistakes. It is important that they know that you know this, and that you tell them they can come to you with any problems or concerns they have. My dear friend and colleague Barbara Levi-Berliner actually recommends sitting down with your middle adolescent and letting him or her know that you will love them no matter what risks they take. She and her husband had a meeting with their 15-year-old son to explicitly talk to him about the risks he might encounter and to tell him that they knew he might be in a situation where he would try alcohol or drugs. They told him they expected him to make mistakes and that they would always be there for him to come home to talk to. Teens may get in trouble with alcohol; they may find themselves in a sexual or romantic relationship they want out of; they may find out they are pregnant or have a sexually transmitted disease. You want to try to make sure that you are the first place they come to for help. The only way to do that is to let them know in advance—probably many times—that you will be there for them no matter what.

When we do not have these types of discussions, our teenagers may be too afraid to come to us when and if they get into trouble. They fear being rejected; they fear the consequences; but probably most importantly, they fear losing your love and respect. I remember being sixteen, pulling out of a parking space and hitting the car behind me when I had only had my driver's license for six months. I panicked, left, and told no one. When my father asked about the bumper, I think I said something like, "someone must have hit me in a parking lot." I think that if I had known it was okay to make a mistake, maybe even expected that in the first six months of driving I might have had an accident, I would have been able to go home and tell my parents. (Sorry Dad…I think he just learned this for the first time!)

This fear of letting parents down can have dramatic repercussions. Many teenage girls ignore signs of pregnancy for months because they are too afraid of what will happen when they tell their parents. Many teenage boys ignore symptoms of sexually transmitted diseases because they are afraid their parents will be angry or lose respect for them. You may remember news stories about teenage girls who carried their pregnancies to term, hiding them from all of the adults in their lives and then killing their newborn infants. More than one-third of teen suicides are gay and lesbian teenagers, who are fatally depressed because they have nowhere to go and are afraid to tell their parents about their orientation—or who have been rejected by their families.

You don't want this to happen to your children. Let them know you will love them no matter what, and that you will always be there for them.

It is also important to share with them that you will make mistakes as a parent. I don't believe that there is any such person as a "perfect parent." I sometimes lose my patience and my temper; I have made decisions that, after time and reflection, I needed to go back and tell my daughter I was wrong about. Don't hesitate to tell your teen, "I'm sorry. I was wrong."

Remember to show affection to your teenager. Respond when they show affection to you. A terrible thing happens around puberty to many boys and girls: Their parents stop showing them any type of physical affection. It is as if parents decide that because their child is developing sexually, they can no longer hug or kiss them because it could be misinterpreted sexually. Many adult women have told me what a loss it was when their fathers stopped hugging or kissing them, almost always without any discussion. They remember wondering what they had done to cause this withdrawal of affection.

Teenagers need physical affection. If you have been hugging them good morning or kissing them good night since they were babies, please do not stop now. I remember an alternative health provider saying human beings need at least five hugs a day. We need physical affection to thrive, and teens denied physical affection may seek it through sex from their dating partners.

Some parents actually ask their teenagers to stop kissing and hugging them. Men often tell me that they have not kissed their fathers or hugged them since they were little boys; more than a few men have shared with me that they only began hugging their father again while he was dying. Please respond to your teen's requests for affection. Hug them back; let them climb in bed with you and snuggle if they want to; continue kissing them good night or good morning.

You *do* want to pay attention to their cues. Many teenagers would die rather than have their parents kiss them in public. Alyssa actually did a science fair experiment about this her last year in middle school. She and a friend monitored whether parents and children kissed good-bye when they were dropped off in the morning at an elementary school and compared it to what happened at the drop-off spot at a middle school. The results weren't surprising: More than half of the elementary school kids kissed their parents good-bye; only a few middle school girls kissed their parents and none of the boys did.

If your child shows you that they no longer welcome physical touch, respect their feelings. But consider telling them that you miss being able to show them physical affection and ask when it might be okay to hug them. You may find that particularly when they are stressed or sad, they still want you to hold them.

One note of caution here. Some parents, particularly men, have told me that they do experience a degree of sexual arousal when they look at their now sexually developed child. It is *never* all right to act on these feelings. Remember that there is a difference between feelings and behaviors. You may not be able to control your thoughts; you are in control of your actions. If these feelings come and go quickly, you can acknowledge them to yourself as passing thoughts. If they continue and you think you might be tempted to act on them, or if you actually experience sexual arousal, please talk to a mental health professional. If you were sexually abused as a teenager yourself, it is particularly important that you seek out this type of help. See the Appendix of this book for resources that can help you.

Facts are not enough. Many parents mistakenly believe that all they need to give their children are the facts about sexuality. Indeed, some parents believe that they have done their job if they give their children a book about growing up and sexuality. Some teens have even told me that in their home, one day a sexuality book mysteriously appeared on their beds or on the kitchen table with no discussion at all. The message: We want you to know about your body and about sex; we just don't want to talk to you about it.

By the time your child is a teenager, you can pretty much assume they have many, if not most of the facts, about human sexuality. Teens do have some pretty strange myths about sex, too. Teens have told me, for example, that a woman can't get pregnant standing up; that Mountain Dew lowers sperm count; and that a woman is most likely to get pregnant when she has her period. Many are short on the details. A 13-year-old girl in one of my groups brazenly told me that many of her friends were "up to fingering." When I asked her what that meant, she mumbled, "You know...touching you down there." When I asked if that referred to touching the clitoris in a purposeful way to orgasm, she responded, "What's a clitoris?"

It is important for you to clarify any misinformation they might have and to make sure they know certain facts. But, it is even more important that you give them your values and an opportunity to discuss their attitudes and feelings.

I'll talk more about this in each of the upcoming chapters, but here's a quick example. Your son who is in the eleventh grade has a steady girlfriend, and he has told you he is in love. You want to talk to him about why you hope he will not engage in sexual intercourse now, and that if he does have intercourse of any kind, why he must use condoms. However, this is not primarily a discussion about the facts of pregnancy, AIDS, and condom use, although you may want to be sure that your teen has access to this information. But what is much more important is talking about your values about premarital sex, his feelings for the young woman and himself, how to know if he is really in love, how to negotiate sexual limits, and so on. And to remind him that you are there for him no matter what he ultimately decides, and that if he ever has a problem or a question, you hope he will want to come to you for assistance.

Do not be afraid of giving mixed messages. I am often asked, "Isn't it a mixed message to tell your teen that you want them to abstain from intercourse and then talk about birth control and condoms?" My answer is, "It is, and we give teenagers complicated messages all the time about their health and futures." For example, we seem as a society to be able to accept that we can tell our teen children that we do not want them to drink, but if they do drink, we want them to call us to pick them up so they don't drive under the influence of alcohol. Indeed, Students Against Destructive Decisions (SADD) promotes contracts between parents and children that say just that. The SADD Massachusetts Chapter has the teen sign a statement that reads, "I pledge my best effort to remain alcohol and drug free. I agree that I will never drive under the influence of either, or accept a ride from someone who is impaired, and I will always wear a seatbelt. Finally I agree to call you if I am ever in a situation that threatens my safety." The parent or other caring adult signs, "I agree to provide for you safe, sober transportation home if you are ever in a situation that threatens your safety and to defer discussion about that decision until a time when we can both discuss the issues in a calm and caring manner." The brochure with the contract says, "The Contract does not condone drinking or using other drugs—it does acknowledge that teens may find themselves in dangerous situations, but they do not deserve to die because of these situations." In other words, I don't want you to drink or do drugs, but if you do, call me and I will help you get home safely. I have never seen the President of SADD having to defend this "double message" on television or in the newspapers.

But, as the President of the Sexuality Information and Education Council of the United States, I was asked this question all the time. Countless advocates who opposed sexuality education said to me, "Talking about abstinence and then talking about contraception gives teens a mixed message. You can't tell them no and then tell them how to do it safely."

I believe that our teenagers can understand that we do not want them to have intercourse (and most, but not all, parents believe that) *and* that we want them to protect themselves and their partner if they do have sexual intercourse, whether we approve or not. We need to give them our clear values about abstinence. In fact, we know from the national adolescent health study that teens who say they know that their parents disapprove of teens having intercourse are less likely to actually have sex. But we also need to be sure that if they are having sexual intercourse of any kind—penile/vaginal, oral, or anal— that they not put themselves at risk of pregnancy or disease. We also, as I said above, want to make sure that they will come to us if they ever suspect they might be pregnant or have a sexually transmitted disease.

Studies indicate that the majority of parents support giving young people information about contraception and condoms, although one in four adults think it is enough to just tell young people that exploring their sexuality outside of marriage is *wrong*. Almost two-thirds of parents agree that young people are going to explore their sexuality as a natural part of growing up, and therefore, the best approach is to provide information and services so that they can act responsibly if they do have intercourse. Sections on abstinence in the upcoming chapters will help parents with different points of view on this issue.

Remember that sexuality education is for both teen boys and teen girls. It is important that you educate both your sons and your daughters. If there are two parents in the home, it is both parents' responsibility to talk to their teenagers about these issues.

In many homes, it is only the girls who receive information about their changing bodies. We prepare our daughters for their first menstruation; we forget to talk to our son about the first seminal emission that will most likely occur while he is sleeping or during masturbation. We talk to our daughters about the importance of abstinence; we say nothing to our sons. Our sons get condoms; our daughters get lectures to "just say no." And so on. In each chapter, I will talk about gender issues during each adolescent period, and ask you to think about the values that you want to give your sons and daughters.

In some homes, it is the mom's job to talk about sexuality, or it is mom's job to talk with the girls and dad's job to talk to the boys. Most of us agree that in adulthood, it is important for men and women to be able to discuss sexuality together, openly and honestly. This is so much easier if both parents model this communication as their children are growing up. Our daughters need to have a chance to hear both men's and women's opinions and points of view; yes, only mom can share what it was like to have cramps, but only dad can share the boy's point of view on asking girls out. Our sons likewise need to hear from people of both sexes. Gay couples raising children as well as single parents need to seek out other adults of the other sex to help play this special role in their child's life.

In families, parents will want to talk about which values they want to give their children about sexuality. This is true whether you are in a couple and raising your children together or separated and divorced but sharing parenting responsibilities. Do not assume that you have the same feelings about these complex and often emotional issues. One of you may be comfortable with masturbation; one of you may not. One of you may be pro-choice; one of you may be pro-life. One of you may be comfortable with your children entertaining their boyfriend or girlfriend in your house when you aren't home; the other may not. And so on. I will give you exercises you can do in your home together to help you figure out what you want to communicate about these issues.

It is not always important for parents to come to consensus about their values, but it is important to give your children a consistent message about their behaviors. Let me explain. Perhaps one of you is pro-choice on the issue of abortion, and one of you believes that abortion is always wrong. Your teenager can certainly understand that people have different views about abortion, and you are modeling that it is possible to love and live with someone with some significant differences in point of view. But if you disagree about the importance of curfews, or whether your child can use alcohol or go to unsupervised parties, you are asking for your child to disobey one of you. On teen behavior questions, you really do need to come to a consensus you can share with your teenager.

It is also important to think through whether you want to give your teen boys and teen girls the *same* values about sexuality. I have a bias here: I think it is important to give boys and girls similar messages. But that does not happen very often. I can't tell you how many times I have had a father say to me, "I worry much more about my girls than I do my boys." One study of parent/teen communication actually found that when moms talked to their sons about sexuality, the boys were more likely to abstain from intercourse. When dads reported that they had talked to their sons about sexuality, the boys were more likely to begin having intercourse. My guess is that the conversations were probably very different! Dads, I am not trying to discourage you from talking here, I just want you to think through your messages.

Make sure your teens have other adults they can go to for information and help about their sexuality. No matter how open you have been with your child about sexuality, they may reach a point where they are not comfortable talking with you, particularly about their own behaviors and questions. It would be a rare situation indeed for a 17-year-old girl to come to her mother and ask, "I'm thinking about having sex. Can you help me find out what to do?" The Search Institute's research found that resilient teenagers have at least three other adults in their lives that they can go to. Think for a minute: Does your teen have a coach, minister, aunt, grandparent, mother of a friend they could go to with a sexuality issue if they didn't want to come to you? How could you help make that happen? And if you are open about sexuality issues, how can you let your teen's friends know that they can always come to you? Many of my colleagues who are professional sexuality educators and who are raising teenagers find themselves in this role with their teen's friends. But, you don't have to be a professional, just a caring, open adult.

Avoid closing down communication with your teenager. It is remarkably easy to say things to your teenager that in effect create barriers to communication. You want to avoid:

- Comparing your teen with other teenagers.
- Lecturing to them.
- Minimizing their problems.
- Talking and not listening.
- "Shoulding" on them: "You should do this...you should feel this..."

In a focus group of teens in Philadelphia, here's what some teens said about their attempts to talk to their parents:

"I've talked to my mom and it's just no, no, no and stuff. I don't talk to her. She talks to me."

"I can't talk to my mom. She doesn't want to talk about it. I tried to bring it up once but she just ignored me."

"You should just listen to what your kids have to say and not lecture and tell them what to do."

"Kids want to be able to ask any question and get the answer— the truth—not beating around the bush."

In a book for adolescent health care providers, Dr. Larry Neinstein advises professionals and parents to avoid saying things such as:

- The trouble with you is…
- How could you do this to me?
- In my day . . .
- You're wrong.
- How could you feel like that?
- That's a dumb thing to say.
- Don't bother me.
- I'm too busy.

Actions speak louder than words. It is one thing to *say* that you are available to talk with your teen about sexuality; it is another thing to *show* them that you really are there for them on these issues. It's one thing to talk about gender equality, but if in your home there are rigid gender roles between the spouses, it teaches something else. It is one thing to tell your teen that only people in committed relationships should have intercourse, and another thing to have them meet your casual lover in the kitchen in the morning. It is one thing to tell them to eat healthily and then to always be on a diet yourself. As we parent throughout our children's lives with us, what we *do* is always more important than what we *say*. Your teenager is watching you for clues about their own behavior. They are also looking to see if you are consistent. Think about what your behaviors are teaching them.

Know what your teenager is being taught about sexuality at school, church, synagogue, or youth group. Many parents have told me that they do not need to talk to their teens about sexuality because there is a sexuality education or health course at church or school or at scouts. These programs can only supplement the education you are providing in your own home. But, first you have to know what's being taught. I will talk more about this in upcoming chapters, but a good sexuality education program recognizes that parents are the primary educator on these issues; gives you a chance to meet the teacher, see the materials, and review the program; and offers homework assignments for you and your child to talk about these issues.

Try to keep up on youth culture. This includes clothes, magazines, music, television, and movies. I remember when I was growing up in the early 1970s that adults were appalled at boys' long hair, girls' unshaved legs, the Doors, Eric Clapton, the Rolling Stones, and certainly our experimenting with drugs and sex. It seems to me that those of us (women) who went braless or (men) who grew our hair shoulder length could be a little more tolerant of purple hair or eyebrow piercings. Some of my baby boomer friends have told me that they shocked themselves the first time they heard Puff Daddy or Nine Inch Nails and thought, "This isn't music...*we* had music!" How much do you know about teen culture? Quick, for a minute, who are Radiohead, Daft Punk, and the Shins? Have you ever watched the television programs *Gossip Girl, The Hills*, or *Flavor of Love*? Did you see the films *Superbad* or *Not Another Teen Movie*? (And these all may be obsolete if you are reading this book a few years from now.) Understanding a little bit about teen culture will allow you to do a better job of communicating with your teenagers. I highly suggest that you at least watch one episode of your teen's favorite television programs. Offer to take your teen to an R-rated movie about teen life that they couldn't get in without you, in exchange for at least a half-hour discussion about any issues it might raise. Let them know that you care about what they are interested in. Remind yourself that if your parents survived the braless hippy look, you really can survive extra piercing. As an aside, understanding teen culture is different than adopting it. I wisely heard someone say last year when mini skirts reappeared, "If you wore them the last time, you are too old to wear them today." Teens want you to know about and respect their culture; they do not want you to dress or act like you are 16.

There is no such thing as too late. I know that some of my readers are pretty worried by now. Your teenager is 13 or 16 or even 19, and you haven't begun to talk about these issues yet. It's okay; not ideal, but okay. It is never too late to begin talking about sexuality. Make a point to start today.

Get help when you need it. It can sometimes feel overwhelming to raise a teenager today. Make sure you have people you can talk to: relatives, friends, other parents, and parent support groups. Clergy, school guidance counselors, psychologists, and mental health providers may also be of help. The Appendix of this book includes organizations, Web sites, and hotlines that can provide additional information and sources of support. Individual counseling for your child and family counseling for your family may all be helpful when situations with your teen begin to career out of control. This book—or any book for that matter—won't be much help for a teen with alcohol or drug problems, a teen who is indiscriminately having sex, or a teen who is on the verge of running away. If you don't know where to start, call the school and ask to talk to the psychologist or social worker who can help you with a referral.

Don't forget to talk about the joys of sexuality. It is so easy in today's world of HIV and AIDS, sexually transmitted diseases, date rape, sexual harassment, homophobia, and so on, to concentrate on the negatives. Remember to emphasize that our sexuality is a wonderful part of life. It is so important that your children know that their bodies are good, that pleasure is good, and that learning about, appreciating, and expressing our sexuality is one of the true joys of adulthood.

This type of open communication is really possible with

your teenager. Here's what some of the other teens in the Pennsylvania focus groups had to say:

> *"My mom's great. We can talk about anything...so I usually do what she thinks is best because I trust her and don't want to disappoint her."*

> *"I talk to my father a lot because we have that kind of open relationship. I can talk to him about anything."*

> *"My mom's pretty cool. Instead of scolding me, she talks to me."*

You can have this type of relationship with your teen about these issues. Let's get started!

Tips for Parents

- Remember that your teenagers want to talk with you about your values.

- Do not have a Big Talk about sexuality.

- You don't have to be comfortable and you don't have to have all the answers.

- Listen to your teenager's point of view.

- Facts are not enough.

- Don't be afraid of giving mixed messages.

- Let your teen know that you expect them to make mistakes and that you will love them no matter what.

- Remember to show affection to your teenager.

- Remember that sexuality education is for both boys and girls.

- Make sure your teens have other adults they can go to for information and help about sexuality.

- Avoid closing down communication with your teenager.

- Actions speak louder than words.

- Know what your teenager is being taught about sexuality at school, church, synagogue, or youth group.

- Try to keep up on youth culture.

- There is no such thing as too late.

- Get help when you need it.

- Talk about the joys of sexuality.

Chapter 2
Adolescence:
An Introduction

Think back to when your child was one or two years old. If you were like me, you were probably avidly reading books that told you how your child would be developing in the next few months. When would Gregory begin to crawl? Was it normal that Alyssa was still using a bottle at age 2? Was it time to start feeding solids? Should I be concerned that my twelve-month-old daughter wasn't walking? There are even best-sellers for parents of infants and toddlers with names like *What to Expect the First Year* and *What to Expect the Toddler Years*. At every visit to the pediatrician, the doctor offered you what pediatricians like to call "anticipatory guidance." They gave you feedback on how your child was reaching important milestones such as talking, walking, using fine motor skills, eating by himself, and following directions. This information was offered to help you anticipate what was likely to come next.

Well, what if I told you that the "developmental milestones" for the adolescent years are just as easy to anticipate?

They are, and in this chapter I will try to help you understand what your child is going to go through during the period from 12 to 21. In 1948, a psychologist named Robert Havighurst defined the "developmental tasks" of adolescence. In any society, he said, there are roles that are expected of individuals at different stages of life. The process of growing to fulfill such roles was defined in 1948 by Havighurst as a "developmental task."

Psychologists and health professionals have divided adolescence into three distinct stages: early adolescence, middle adolescence, and late adolescence. Understanding these stages, and being able to assess where your teen is in their development, will help you understand your teen's behavior and his or her developing sexuality.

Before I begin to describe these stages, you need to know that there is no such thing as an average or normal adolescent. Individual adolescents vary widely in the pace of their development. Simple chronological age won't tell you much about where your child is developmentally. In any group of 13-year-old teens, some will still seem mostly like children and others may behave like mature teens. Even the same teenager may be more mature in some areas and less mature in others. For example, a 14-year-old young woman may have reached full physical development but might still act emotionally like a teen a few years younger. Or a 15-year-old boy may have advanced thinking skills but may only be beginning puberty. Conversely, a physically mature 15-year-old boy might look like an adult, might function emotionally as a 12-year-old boy when dealing with his parents or teachers, but may be experimenting sexually with both girls and boys. For most teenagers development unfolds on several levels, so don't be surprised if you see your own teen in several different levels of development as I describe the stages.

Many adults assume that adolescence is necessarily a time of turmoil and upset. This notion can actually be traced back to 1904, when a psychologist named G. Stanley Hall published a book called *Adolescence*. He wrote that adolescence is a period of "Sturm und Drang," or storm and stress. He described adolescence as a turbulent, transitional stage where the emotional life of the adolescent swings between wild extremes.

We now know differently. According to the Institute of Medicine, "Most young people move through their adolescent years without experiencing great trauma or getting into serious trouble." The National Research Council's Forum on Adolescence calls adolescence "a time of both tremendous opportunity and risk." More than eight in ten teenagers cope pretty well with the challenges of adolescence, and about one-third of all teenagers find their teenage years a breeze.

Physical development, including sexual maturation, is the most obvious area of development for you to see. During adolescence, your child will mature into a biological adult with the physical capacity for reproduction and sexual intimacy. This physical development is greatest during the period of early adolescence called puberty, and I'll talk more about it in the section called Early Adolescence on page 57. Many readers' teen children will have already passed through puberty, and you may want to only skim that section to understand some of the emotional issues of early adolescence.

Let me clarify some of these words for a moment. "Puberty," "teenager," and "adolescence" are not interchangeable terms. Puberty is the stage of physical development when a human being becomes capable of sexual reproduction. Teenagers are defined by chronological age: A teenager is a young person between the ages of 13 and 19. You may be surprised to know that the term "teenager" was coined in the 1930s in America and was widely disliked by teens themselves because they saw it as derogatory.

Adolescence is a relatively new concept historically. The word adolescence derives from the Latin verb "adolescere," meaning to "grow up." Prior to the early twentieth century, and still today in many developing countries, children marry or form sexual unions at the time of or shortly after puberty, and begin their adult family and work responsibilities almost immediately. Puberty has obviously always occurred to human beings, but the concept of a separate stage of life between childhood and adulthood seems to have been invented between 1900 and 1920. During these years, new labor laws were passed that severely limited hiring children to work. As a result, by 1920, secondary education had become more important. It may surprise you to know that in 1900, only 6.4 percent of young people graduated from high school; by 1956, 62.3 percent graduated from high school; today, it is close to 90 percent, although in some areas, as many as one-third of high school freshmen don't graduate. The 1920s flapper and her raccoon coat–sporting boyfriend were the country's first real teenagers.

In America and other westernized societies, adolescence is now the period from puberty through the attainment of full adult responsibilities. And increasingly, it doesn't end until one's mid to late twenties. I recently saw a birthday card that captured America's ambivalence about assuming adult responsibilities. It said something like:

13–19 . . . .*adolescence*

20–29 . . . . . .*adolescence*

30–45 . . . . . .*adolescence*

45 and up . . . .*late adolescence!*

The Five I's of Adolescent Development

According to psychologists, all adolescents have to accomplish five major developmental tasks in addition to physically maturing into an adult. In order to help me remember these tasks in graduate school, I named them the five "I's" of adolescent development: Intellect, Independence, Identity, Integrity, and Intimacy. Let me explain.

Intellect

Teenagers develop intellectually over the course of adolescence. Children and very young adolescents are concrete thinkers, and focus on real objects, present actions, and immediate benefits. For example, my son Gregory at age 6 could hardly think on Monday about what he might like to do the coming weekend; when I asked him what kind of camp he might like to go to that summer, he couldn't imagine when that would be. New research on the brain demonstrates that the prefrontal cortex is developing until the late teens and early twenties.

Concrete thinkers have difficulty projecting themselves into the future. Just for a minute try to remember yourself as a child and how long it seemed to take from the first day of school in September until Christmas vacation. Today, those four months from Labor Day to New Year's probably fly by. During adolescence, young people develop a greater ability to think abstractly, plan for their future, and understand the impact of their current actions on their future lives and other people.

Developmental Tasks of Adolescence: The Five "I's"

- Intellect
- Independence
- Identity
- Integrity
- Intimacy

The ability to think abstractly is part of the foundation for a sexually healthy adolescence and adulthood. Young people, and indeed adults, need to think through the consequences of their actions. One of the most important life behaviors of a sexually healthy person is the ability to understand that there is a difference between having sexual feelings and acting upon them. Indeed, we want people to be able to distinguish between sexual behaviors that are life enhancing and those that might be destructive to themselves or others.

This is a lesson that too many adults have not learned. Think for a moment about Jim Baker, Marv Albert, Pee Wee Herman, Frank Gifford, and Bill Clinton.

Young people who are still concrete thinkers are going to have trouble thinking through the potential consequences of their sexual decisions. They can recognize that they are having sexual feelings, but they will be unlikely to be able to plan for sexual relationships. They will have difficulty anticipating the consequences, clearly articulating their values, negotiating sexual limits with a partner, and obtaining contraception and condoms in advance of intercourse. In fact, the research is very clear about young teens inability to plan for sex: The younger teens are when they begin to have sexual intercourse, the less likely they are to use a contraceptive method.

Even more importantly, concrete thinkers do not have the intellectual capacity to see a situation from another person's perspective. This ability for "social cognition" is the foundation for relationships that are mutually caring of both partners' feelings. This lack of social cognition helps explain how early adolescents can break up with each other so easily without seeming regard for the other teen's feelings. Empathy develops during adolescence.

As I will talk about in coming chapters, this inability to

prepare for future consequences is why it is so important for you as the parent to help your middle school and perhaps even early high school age child avoid situations where they have not thought through the consequences—and where sexual feelings are likely to move too quickly into behaviors that they are not ready for. Roleplaying with your concrete-thinking early adolescent can help prepare them for difficult situations. You might say, "Tell me what you might say if someone offers you a beer." "Tell me what you will do if you are at the mall and you see one of your friends shoplift something." "If your girlfriend starts pressuring you to move beyond kissing, what might you say?" By talking through these situations in advance, your child will be better prepared to deal with them if they do arise.

Independence

By the end of adolescence, your child will need to become *independent*. Picture your own life in ten years. Does it involve having your teenager live at home with you, with you still providing all of their financial support, cooking, laundry, the car? For most of us, the answer is *no*. We want our children to become independent adults with lives of their own. Yet more and more young people in their early twenties are living in their parent's home or are financially dependent on their parents. In one recent study that I read, more than one in two young people between 18 and 24 were living at home with their parents. One in ten people ages 25 to 34 still live with their parents.

The ultimate goal of adolescence is *adulthood*: emotional, psychological, and financial independence from parents. And that means your teen—even at ages 12 and 13—needs to start pulling away from you. This move to independence is one of the reasons that there are so many parent-child struggles during adolescence. Sometimes when Alyssa and I are getting into it over some issue, I remind myself, "This is good. I want her to grow up to be an independent adult. She has to be doing this!"

The parent-child relationship is transformed during adolescence. You are no longer the all-powerful, all-knowing presence in your child's life, if you ever were! But it is important to know that only about one in six teenagers and their parents will experience a severe disruption in the parent-child relationship. It is true that adolescents have to begin separating from their parents, but most teenagers also still look to their parents and families for guidance and support.

The move to independence can be confusing for both parents and their teen children. One day, your teen wants to cuddle with you before bedtime; the next day they are slamming their bedroom door, yelling, "You wouldn't understand!" One day, they want your guidance and help; the next day, they won't go to a movie with you because someone might see them with their parents. Your job is to be there when they do want you and try to support their moves to independence. As my friend and colleague Bob Selverstone wrote, "It is fine for the child to walk away from the parent—you are preparing them for a life on their own. You must assure them that you won't walk away from them."

Identity

Adolescents have to develop their *identity*. They are beginning to prepare themselves for adult roles in society. In 1968, psychologist Erik Erikson labeled this the "crisis of identity." He said that the combination of physical growth, emotional maturation, and social responsibility in adolescence causes the young person to seek the answer to the question, "Who Am I?"

This search for identity includes "functional identity," "conceptual identity," and "sexual self-concept."

Teens must seek their "functional identity": They need to think about how they will support themselves and contribute to their own families and society in adulthood. They are trying on the possibility of jobs and careers. When Alyssa was 14, she told us that she might want to be a photographer for *National Geographic*, an archeologist, or an attorney. Right now, everything seems possible, and her interests are vast. By the end of late adolescence, she is likely to have a much better sense of what she sees for herself in terms of a vocation—or at least we hope so for her!

The search for identity also involves the more complex process of developing a "conceptual identity": Adolescents are beginning to understand how they fit into the religious, cultural, ethnic, moral, and political constructs of their environments. They are able to affirm, for example, "I am a Christian, African-American, Democrat from a working-class family" and understand more about what that means.

Part of developing a conceptual identity is developing a sense of a "sexual self-concept." One's sexual self-concept is how an individual evaluates his or her sexual feelings and attractions. It includes both gender identity and sexual orientation.

During adolescence, young people develop a stronger sense of their gender identity. Gender identity includes how one understands that one is male or female, and the roles, values, duties, and responsibilities of being a man or a woman. Most young people have a firm sense of their maleness or femaleness prior to adolescence, but it is in adolescence that clear identification with adult masculine and feminine roles emerges. (Some young people begin to identify themselves as "transgender" during adolescence: I will discuss this in greater depth in Chapter Six.)

I believe strongly that rigid gender-role stereotypes hurt both young men and young women. They limit their choice of classes in school, their goals for the future, and their sense of themselves as sexual persons. Indeed, I also believe that gender-role stereotypes place them at risk of unintended pregnancy and sexually transmitted diseases. Young women too often learn that "It is better to be cute and popular than smart," that "Girls have few sexual feelings," and that "Girls who prepare for sex are bad." Boys may be learning that "Real men always want sex" and that "Guys should never act like girls." One study found that teenage boys who agree with traditional cultural messages about masculinity are less likely than other young men to use condoms consistently (if at all), and are more likely to say that if they made a partner pregnant, they would feel like a "real man." They are less likely to think that men share the responsibility for preventing pregnancy.

During adolescence, young people develop a greater understanding of their own sexual orientation. Although many gay and lesbian adults say that they were aware that there was something different about them at an early age, it is during adolescence that young people become more aware of their sexual attractions and love interests, and adultlike erotic feelings emerge. In one study of students in grades seven to twelve, 88 percent of teenagers described themselves as predominately heterosexual, 1 percent described themselves as bisexual or predominately homosexual, and 11 percent were "unsure" of their sexual orientation. But during the course of the adolescent years, uncertainty about sexual orientation lessens: More than one in four 12 year olds are "unsure" about their sexual orientation compared with only 5 percent of 18 year olds. In a study of gay and bisexual men who were 21 years old or younger, the mean age of self-awareness about their personal sexual orientation was 14.9 years, and the mean age to come out to others was 16.5 years of age. I will discuss more about sexual orientation in Chapter Five.

Integrity

During adolescence, teens also need to develop their own sense of integrity. Teenagers are testing and developing a sense of their own values. They need to identify their values, and decide what is personally right for them. They need to understand the intense peer and media pressures to be popular and accepted, and they need to learn to make decisions consistent with their own values and choices, even if that means going against their friends.

Adolescence is often a time to test out values that are different than one's parents and family. Many teenagers go through a period of seeming to reject their parents' values, yet almost all of them ultimately adopt values pretty similar to their parents by the time they reach adulthood. Do you remember the television sitcom *Family Ties* from the 1980s? Young Alex, played by Michael J. Fox, was a capitalist Republican in a home of baby boomer, liberal, former-hippy parents. Well, if this were real life, by the time he finished college, he would probably have affirmed more progressive values similar to his parents. Try not to be alarmed when your teenager announces that she is a Buddhist, a socialist, a vegetarian, or an advocate for capital punishment, whatever it is your family values might contradict. It is likely to pass!

Intimacy

During adolescence, your child will develop the capacity for intimacy, and most teens will experience their first mature love relationship. It is during adolescence that most of us fall in love for the first time, that most of us fall out of love or have our hearts broken, and that we learn about true friendship. Despite what some adults think, these love relationships are not "puppy love," and parents need to take their teen child's being in love seriously. Your early teen may spend hours daydreaming or talking on the phone with a boyfriend or girlfriend. Your middle teen may want to spend hours with a boyfriend or girlfriend and is probably experimenting with showing that love with some kinds of sexual behaviors. Your late adolescent may be planning a future with that person. Love relationships are different at each stage of adolescence, and I will discuss them in upcoming chapters.

For now though, I want you to take a moment and think about *your* first love. What was his or her first name? How old were you? How did you feel about him or her? How did it feel when he or she called you on the phone? Smiled at you? Held your hand? Do you remember having a crush on someone who did not like you back? How did that feel? How do you remember feeling when you broke up with your beloved? How do you remember your own parents dealing with the teenage you in love?

Most of us remember those feelings quite intensely. And for many people, that first love may be one of the most intoxicating of their life. And for sure, it is one we never forget.

The Three Stages of Adolescence

In addition to outlining the developmental tasks of adolescence, developmental psychologists and health professionals have categorized adolescence into three distinct stages. They are *early adolescence*, *middle adolescence*, and *late adolescence*. In this section, I will briefly introduce these stages, but I will talk more about them in the upcoming chapters that are divided by age. Remember again as you read these that there is no such thing as an "average adolescent," and that your teen might be in different stages of adolescent development on different developmental tasks.

Early Adolescence

Early adolescence typically occurs for girls between ages 9 and 13 and between ages 11 and 15 for boys. That means that most girls are likely to be going through the early adolescent period between fourth and eighth grade, while boys are several years behind in development, going through early adolescence between sixth and tenth grades. But some teenagers do not biologically become early adolescents until their junior or senior year in high school. The process of puberty from the first physical changes to obtaining a fully adult body may take as few as one to two years or as many as four or five years. Both are normal. On average, boys begin and end puberty about a year to two years later than girls do.

Puberty

Puberty, the biological transition from childhood to adulthood, is the defining characteristic of the early adolescent period. The early adolescent experiences more rapid body changes than at any time in the lifespan except infancy. Both boys and girls grow rapidly during the early adolescent years. This is known as the growth spurt, and it lasts between two and three years. Growth accounts for about one-fourth of final adult height. On average, girls have their growth spurt about two years before similarly aged boys; that's why the sixth and seventh grade girls tower over the boys in the class picture. In general, girls grow the most at age 12; boys at age 14. Most girls will grow the most in the year before their first period, and continued growth after that is limited. Weight gain accompanies height growth: Pubertal weight gain accounts for about half of an individual's ideal adult body weight.

Both boys and girls develop what are called "secondary sexual characteristics" during puberty. They get pubic and underarm hair; their voices deepen; and they develop sweat glands in their genital and underarm areas that produce body odor. You may need to remind your early adolescent that they need to take a shower daily, and it's time to introduce them to deodorant.

Girls begin sexual development earlier than boys. Breast budding is the first sign of puberty—the breasts begin to elevate as small mounds. A 1996 study of more than seventeen thousand girls, found that on average African-American girls start breast budding just before age 9, and white girls start about the age of 10. However, average means that half of girls start this process earlier, and half will begin it later. It is not unusual then and nothing to worry about if your daughter doesn't have breast buds until the seventh or eighth grade—or if she began these changes in the second or third grade. During puberty, the breasts develop to near their adult size, and the uterus and ovaries grow up to seven times their childhood size. The vagina, clitoris, and labia also grow in size.

Girls today are having their first periods at earlier ages than girls did in the 1960s. A girl's first period is likely to come about two years after breast buds first develop and underarm hair appears, but this isn't always the case. Make sure you have had several discussions about what to do when your daughter gets her first period once you have noticed breast budding. The average age for first menstruation (known by doctors as *menarche*, pronounced MEN-ar-key) is about 12.5 years, but some girls don't begin their first period until age 16.5. In other words, about half of all girls will have their periods before the end of seventh grade, and many will begin while they are still in elementary school. It also means that about half of girls will be in at least the eighth grade before their first period, and some may be as old as juniors in high school. All of these are normal.

Male sexual development generally begins at an average age of 11.5, with a normal range of 9 to 14 years. In almost all boys, testicular enlargement is the first sign of puberty, something most parents are unlikely to observe! During puberty, the testes, epididymis, and the prostate increase seven times the childhood size, and the penis usually doubles in size. First ejaculation, also known by sexologists as *semenarche* to indicate its correspondence with menarche, generally happens midway through pubertal development. Boys often experience their first ejaculation as a nocturnal emission, or wet dream. And just as it is important to prepare your daughter for her first period, it is important to prepare boys for their first nocturnal emission. In general, it takes boys about three years from the first signs of puberty to reach full physical adult status, but in some boys, it may take as short as two years or as long as five years. Both are normal.

Preparing your son or daughter for puberty is very important. Remember a Big Talk isn't likely to work. Try to have little talks with them during their late elementary school and middle school years. Share with them your own memories of going through these dramatic changes. Talk to your daughter about what to do if she starts her first period when she is away from home. It is a good idea for a girl who has had her growth spurt to carry a sanitary pad with her in her backpack. Be sure to talk with your son about the changes he will experience in penis and testicular size, and about the probability that as he develops, he may have wet dreams. Tell him you will understand if you come across stained sheets or ask him to put the sheets in the laundry basket. Better yet, have him start doing his own laundry, a good skill for later life!

Boys in middle school are often quite concerned about penis size. In a class I taught a few years ago to eighth graders, questions about penis size came up almost weekly in the anonymous question box I had in the classroom, even though we had covered the information pretty thoroughly in a formal session weeks ago. Boys this age need to know that the average adult penis is two to four inches flaccid and five to seven inches erect. They need to know that some men are "showers" and some men are "growers": Men who are smaller while they are flaccid have penises that grow longer when they are sexually excited; bigger flaccid penises grow less during an erection. And they need to know that penis size doesn't matter for sexual satisfaction most of the time.

Boys in middle school need to know about erections. Now, I hope you have read my first book, *From Diapers to Dating*, and you have been educating your son about erections since preschool days. If so, you don't need to say much more than, "You will have erections more frequently as you go through puberty." But if you have not been doing this all along, you may need to have some more detailed discussions.

As boys go through puberty, they are likely to begin to be more interested in sex, and more likely to feel sexual attraction. Their penises become erect more often, often quite unexpectedly and at unwelcome times. I once read in a conservative magazine that teens should resist all activities that might cause them to experience genital arousal; uh oh, I thought, there goes the lunchroom! It takes very little for a teen boy to get an erection: a sexy ad, a suggestive music video, a girl bending over to pick up a fork, someone attractive smiling at him while he's giving a speech in English class. Boys need to know that this is a perfectly normal response and that the erection will go away by itself. Despite what some boys have been told, there is no medical condition known as "blue balls"; erections do subside by themselves. Nevertheless, a discussion with dad or some other man in his life about what to do so that others don't know he is aroused could be face saving: Moving the lunch tray or books to a strategic place or holding books or papers at waist level can help.

Girls this age often worry about breast size. The girls with larger breasts than their friends often hunch over, as if they want to hide them. Girls with smaller breasts worry that they will never grow. Other girls worry that their breasts are not exactly the same size, a perfectly normal variation. Middle school girls need to know that breast size is highly individual and genetic: She is likely to be similar in size to her mother, aunts, or grandmothers. There is not much that can be done to increase breast size. The exercises that I did as a 12-year-old—"We must, we must, we must build up our bust"—do not work. Very thin girls can be advised that gaining weight can help. As an adolescent medicine doctor told the daughter of a friend of mine, "There is no fat on your body. Breasts are primarily fat. Gain ten pounds this year, and I'm pretty sure your breasts will get a little bigger."

On the other hand, some boys are troubled by a growth in glandular tissue around their breasts, a condition called "gynecomastia." These boys sometimes worry that they are growing breasts or even turning into a girl. Nearly one in five boys will experience some breast tissue development. In most boys, this is just a variation of male pubertal development, and usually resolves itself in a year to a year and a half. If your son seems very bothered by this or it doesn't go away in a couple of years, talk to your physician.

You can get help in educating your middle school student about puberty. Ask your pediatrician to talk to you at your child's next annual exam. Your pediatrician can tell you how developed your son or daughter is. Many pediatricians or adolescent medicine doctors use something called a Tanner Scale to rate physical sexual development in both boys and girls. See the box on adolescent physical development on page 63. There are also excellent books and videos about body changes for boys and girls; I have listed some of them in the last chapter. Scout troops, church and synagogue groups, and community agencies may also have programs on preparing for puberty. You may also want to read the longer sections on preparing your sons and daughters for puberty in the first book in this series, *From Diapers to Dating: A Parent's Guide to Raising Sexually Healthy Children*.

Some teenagers do not begin puberty until high school. As slow developers, they may be teased and they may feel left out. They may wonder if they are normal. If a boy has no pubic hair by age 15 or a girl has none by age 14, it is time to bring them to an adolescent medicine expert for an evaluation. Likewise, if a girl has not had her first period five years after her breasts budded, she needs to be evaluated. The doctor will want to rule out hypothalamic, pituitary, and gonadal dysfunction and undetected chronic illnesses. In more than 60 percent of cases of delayed puberty, however, the cause is genetic not medical. Try to remember if you developed later than your peers; find out when your parents went through puberty. Still, if your teen who is in their junior or senior year of high school has yet to begin puberty, make an appointment for your child to see a health care provider.

Adolescent Physical Development: The Tanner Stages			
Tanner Stage	Pubic Hair	Breasts (female)	Penis/Scrotum (male)
1	None	Childlike	Childlike
2	Sparse	Breast buds	Scrotum turns red; penis childlike
3	Darker, begins to curl	Breasts and nipples enlarge	Penis length increases, scrotum continues to enlarge and darken
4	Coarse, curly, less than adult	Continued breast development	Penis increases in length and circumference
5	Adult	Adult	Adult

Emotional changes of early adolescence

Adjusting to the dramatic changes in their bodies is not easy for early adolescents. Your early adolescent may seem obsessed with his or her body image and spend hours in front of the mirror. Getting dressed for school or church can be pure torture, both for the teen and the parent waiting in the car. Teens at this stage are self-preoccupied, and almost all worry about their appearance and whether they appear attractive. They also worry incessantly about whether their clothes and hair are "right" and whether their friends will accept them.

Early adolescents want to know, "Am I normal?" They are concerned about their height, their weight, their breast or penis size, and whether they are too developed or too underdeveloped. They compare themselves frequently to their friends: Why is it that Susie has bigger breasts or that John seems so tall? They wonder whether their feelings, which may be fluctuating immensely, are normal. It is so important for parents to reassure their early adolescent children that they are normal and that they are developing according to their own personal, genetically predetermined timetable.

These physical changes also bring about enormous emotional changes. Fluctuating hormones often lead to extreme moodiness and unexplainable feelings. Many parents report that their early teen is experiencing wide mood and behavior swings. It is during the period right before and shortly after puberty that conflicts with parents seem to peak. Early adolescents are often very resistant to advice or criticism from parents. They will test authority and boundaries often as they attempt to begin to separate from their parents.

Friends become more important during early and middle adolescence, and being popular becomes of the utmost importance. The good news is that needing to be just like your friends, known by psychologists as "conformity with peers," peaks in early adolescence, and then starts to decline during the older teen years. The bad news is that peer pressure can be intense during these years, and it influences everything from what kind of sneakers are okay, to whether a teen can go to a restaurant with a parent, to whether your child will become involved in smoking cigarettes, drinking, or experimenting with sexual behaviors. I will talk more about this in the next chapter.

Best friends are common with both boy and girl early adolescents. Teens at this age are likely to primarily have same-sex friendships, with some contact with the other gender in groups of friends.

Early adolescents are also developing intellectually. They are beginning to develop the capacity to reason abstractly, and this means that they will spend a good deal of time turning inward. Teens at this age often spend a great deal of time day-dreaming. Many parents have told me that they are worried about the amount of time their early adolescent spends alone in his or her room; not to worry, this is normal, expected, and even important for their development. Many teens turn to journals or diaries to record their intense feelings; parents need to respect their privacy to do so.

Teens at this age often feel that they are onstage and that everyone is looking at them; psychologists describe early ado-lescents as having an "imaginary audience." It is not unusual for early adolescents to be highly dramatic, believing that they alone in the history of the universe are experiencing these types of feelings, and that their problems are unique. It is important to acknowledge the intensity of your child's feelings and not try to minimize them. Better to say, "I know you're having a really tough time today; why don't you go to your room and write in your journal," than, "Stop being such a drama queen and get down here and help me."

Middle Adolescence

Ask someone to describe a typical adolescent, and they will probably describe someone who is in middle adolescence. For girls, middle adolescence generally occurs between ages 13 and 16; for boys, it generally occurs between ages 14 and 17. It is the stage when teenagers begin to look like and act more like "typical teens." It is also the stage when teens are likely to rely more on their friends than on their parents, and to adopt the teen culture of their preferred social group.

When I was first trained in adolescent health care, I was taught that middle adolescents think of themselves as invul-nerable and immortal. Indeed, middle adolescents are often described as feeling omniscient (all knowing), omnipotent (all powerful), and invincible (nothing can hurt them). Many teenagers do take risks, because they believe "nothing bad can happen to me." They think, "I can drive 90 miles an hour because I won't have an accident," or, "I'm too young to get pregnant so I don't need to use birth control."

However, research during the past twenty years has demonstrated conclusively that on the whole adolescents are not more likely to think they are invulnerable to risks than adults. In other words, some adolescents and some adults are more likely to take greater risks than others.

Think about yourself for a moment. In general, I am pretty risk-averse. I wear my seat belt and drive the speed limit at all times, would not consider driving under the influence of alcohol, and stay away from all sports activities where I could get seriously hurt. But a lot of my friends ski and snowboard, enjoy driving quickly, and invest heavily in technology stocks. We have different approaches to risk taking. So do teenagers.

Risk taking is not all bad. The Institute of Medicine's report on adolescence, "Risks and Opportunities," reminds scientists that risk taking involves exploration, imagination, new relationships, testing new levels of independence, developing new values, and unleashing creativity. These are all pretty positive qualities. The question that I will talk more about in Chapter Five on grades eleven and twelve is how parents can help protect these risk takers enough to not do something that will endanger their lives or futures. Helping your teens assess how risky a behavior is can help.

During middle adolescence, teens want increased independence from their families, and the peer group is going to be increasingly important. Your teen's friends are likely to change during this period, as middle adolescents seek other teens who are perhaps more like them than their childhood friends. Teens at this time are often intensely involved with a group of friends, rather than the single best friends of a few years ago. It is the peer group that affirms teens' images of themselves: By being accepted or rejected by certain groups, they learn more about who they are and the way they see themselves. Expect that your middle adolescent will want to dress like, listen to the same music as, and develop the same outside interests as their friends.

Pay attention to who your teen is choosing as friends and what this can tell you about your own child. If your teen is hanging out with genuinely "good kids," they are likely to support each other. If your teen is hanging out with kids who you can tell are involved with drinking and drugs, it is naïve to think that only your teen isn't involved. The good news though for parents is that despite the influence of friends on day-to-day decisions, teens still want parents involved in helping them make important long-term decisions such as education and career preparation.

Teens in middle adolescence can be very narcissistic—the world revolves around them. Your middle adolescent may seem selfish as well as self-absorbed. They can be tough to live with, as they seem to forget how to pick up their clothes in the bathroom, do their chores, or attend an event on your family calendar. They are unlikely to remember to be empathetic to you. One night when Alyssa was a teen, after I returned from a business trip, she waited up to talk to me about what had been going on in her life. She spilled news with great gusto for more than an hour. I said to her, "Honey, are you going to ask me about my trip?" She responded, "No, mom, this is about *me!*"

During middle adolescence, many teens develop the capacity for abstract thinking. I love talking with Greg these days about ideas: He is able to grasp new concepts and apply them in new ways. Middle adolescents experience a new set of feelings, including the ability to empathize and understand the feelings of others. It is a time of increased intellectual ability and creativity. It is also the time when teens may begin to understand their own personal limitations, which can lead to decreased self-esteem, depression, anxiety, and eating disorders in some teens.

More to the point of this book, sexuality, relationships, and sexual expression are of major importance in the lives of many middle adolescents. Most teenagers fall in love for the first time during these years. Most begin to have a stronger sense of themselves as sexual beings. Most middle adolescents will have their first boyfriend or girlfriend, and most will begin to experiment with sexual behaviors. Most will develop an understanding of their sexual orientation—whether they are homosexual, heterosexual, or bisexual. They also develop a greater understanding of their gender identity.

The average age for first intercourse in the United States is middle adolescence. On average, teen boys have sexual intercourse for the first time at age 16; on average, teen girls have their first sexual intercourse at age 17. I'll help you deal with this more explicitly in upcoming chapters.

A friend recently sent me an online message called "The Cat Years" that summed up middle adolescence pretty well. It said the author was unknown. The person wrote:

> I just realized that while children are dogs—loyal and affectionate—teenagers are cats. It's so easy to be a dog owner. You feed it, train it, boss it around. It puts its head on your knee and gazes at you as if you were a painting. It bounds indoors with enthusiasm when you call it.
>
> Then around age 13, your adoring little puppy turns into a big old cat. When you tell it to come inside, it looks amazed, as

if wondering who died and made you emperor. Instead of dogging your footsteps, it disappears. You won't see it until it gets hungry, when it turns up its nose at whatever you are serving. When you reach out to ruffle its head, in an old affectionate gesture, it twists away from you, then gives you a blank stare, as if trying to remember where it has seen you before.

You, not realizing that the dog is now a cat, think something must be desperately wrong with it. It seems so antisocial, so distant, sort of depressed. It won't go on family outings. Since you're the one who raised it, taught it to fetch and stay and sit on command, you assume you did something wrong. Flooded with guilt and fear, you redouble your efforts to make your pet behave.

Only now, you're dealing with a cat, so that everything that worked before, now produces the opposite of the desired result. Call it, and it runs away. Tell it to sit, and it jumps on the counter. The more you go toward it, the more it moves away.

Instead of continuing to act like a dog owner, you need to learn to behave like a cat owner. Put a dish of food near the door, and let it come to you. But remember that your cat needs your help and your affection, too. Sit still, and it will come, seeking that warm comforting lap that it has not entirely forgotten. Be there to open the door for it.

Late Adolescence

The Internet message ends with the transition to late adolescence. It says, "One day, your almost-grown-up child will walk into the kitchen, give you a big kiss, and say, 'You've been on your feet all day. Let me do the dishes for you.' Then you'll realize your cat is a dog again."

Many parents breathe a sigh of relief in late adolescence. They feel that they are getting their children "back." Late adolescence is the stage where young people move toward adult roles and responsibilities. It generally begins in girls at around ages 16 to 18, and in boys around ages 17 and 18. It is hard to know in the United States and other western countries when adolescence ends today. Many young people delay assuming adult roles by extending their educations, continuing to live in their parents' homes, traveling, and generally avoiding the adult responsibilities of jobs and families. In fact, at the turn of the twenty-first century, young people are delaying adult responsibilities longer than at any time in our history. For example, the median age at first marriage is at its highest ever in the United States; it has gone from a low of 20 for young women and 22.5 for young men in 1956 to a high in 2005 of about 27 for men and 26 for women. I know some people in their late twenties or thirties who are still wrestling with the emotional issues of late adolescence!

By late adolescence, physical maturation is complete. Young people have reached their full adult height; their secondary sexual characteristics like breast and penis size are almost fixed; and they generally look like the adults they will be. Body image, gender-role identification, and sexual orientation are pretty well established. Late adolescents generally feel pretty comfortable with their bodies, although eating disorders are now a major problem on college campuses for both young men and young women.

Intellectually, late adolescents have reached their highest level of thinking. Most will be able to engage in abstract thinking, being able to separate what is possible from what is real. Teens at this stage become more aware of how their past and present decisions will affect their futures. Most late adolescents are able to understand and plan for the consequences of their actions and their decisions. They have the ability to compromise, and they can set limits for their own behaviors. They have developed a sense of their own values and know what is important to them. They have developed a strong conscience, and a sense of perspective.

Some teens at 19 and 20 have difficulty moving into this last period of adolescence. Late adolescents are more aware of their own personal strengths and weaknesses. Recognizing personal limitations may lead to depression, suicidal tendencies, and other emotional disorders. In addition, certain mental illnesses like schizophrenia and bipolar disease often have their onset during these years. Do not hesitate to reach out for professional assistance for your older teens if they seem to be having difficulty coping.

This is also the period when adolescents often leave their parents' homes to go to college or begin working. Most late adolescents begin to develop realistic vocational goals. Some late adolescents begin to work (half of all teens ages 18 to 19 have a job); some marry (2 percent of girls and 6 percent of boys ages 18 and 19); and about twenty thousand serve in the military. Many develop intense love relationships with another person, often their first (and for some their final) mature love. It is the time when we as parents have to let go of our children and let them become adults, a process that is not as easy as it sounds.

One of the best parts of late adolescence is that many parents report a new, more adultlike relationship with their teen. Peers once again become less important in determining behavior, and teens move to a more adult-to-adult relationship with their parents. They can once again just hang out with their parents, sharing ideas and thoughts. You may have heard the joke about the young man who returns from his first semester at college and asks his parents, "How come you've gotten so much smarter while I was away this semester?" He is telling them that he is ready to be part of their lives again, but in a new and different way. In the words of the e-mail message, your dog is back!

Values Exercise for Chapter Three

Your eighth-grade daughter comes to breakfast on a school day wearing a thigh high skirt and a tight T-shirt that shows her navel when she breathes. You:

❏ a) Smile and say nothing.
❏ b) Tell her to go change.
❏ c) Ask her what message she is trying to give with her clothes.
❏ d) Wonder what happened to your little girl.

Your seventh grader has started hanging out with a friend you do not like. You:

❏ a) Forbid her/him to see that friend.
❏ b) Invite the friend over to get to know her/him better.
❏ c) Ignore it; most of your teen's friends are nice.
❏ d) Sit down and talk with your child.

You walk into the living room and find your eighth grader engaged in some pretty heavy kissing with his or her boyfriend/girlfriend. You:

❏ a) Cough loudly and hope they hear you and stop.
❏ b) Walk out quietly and hope they didn't see you.
❏ c) Say, "Not in my house, not with my son/daughter. It's time to leave."
❏ d) Ask them to discuss with you their behaviors and the importance of setting sexual limits.

You walk into the playroom and see that your 12-year-old teen is looking at adult sex sites on the Internet. You:

❏ a) Turn off the computer and take away Internet privileges for a month.
❏ b) Say nothing and leave him/her to exploring. After all, curiosity is okay.
❏ c) Remind him/her about your rules for Internet use.
❏ d) Have a discussion with him/her about erotica and your feelings about Internet sex sites.

Chapter 3
The Middle School Years

Starting Middle School

I distinctly remember my first day of junior high school. I was terrified. I was leaving the top grade of the elementary school I had been at for four years. I was afraid of meeting new children, of changing classes, of the hall, and particularly of having to change clothes in gym. I had heard rumors about the girls' locker room and what it was like to have to take showers after gym class. I was going into the seventh grade.

Today's middle school is likely to begin in fifth or sixth grade and go through eighth grade. Schools set aside just for early adolescents are a relatively new concept. My parents went to grammar school, which went from first to eighth grade. Junior high schools didn't become popular until 1945. The move from junior high schools (which went from seventh to ninth grades) to middle school began as a reform movement in the 1960s. During the past thirty years, the number of middle schools has increased dramatically, and the number of junior high schools has plummeted to only a little more than a thousand nationwide.

I am frankly not crazy about middle schools. Putting prepubescent 10- and 11-year-olds into a school with postpubescent 13-year-olds just does not seem like a very good idea to me. Today's 10- and 11-year-olds are being exposed to some issues that most of us couldn't fathom when we were that age. School administrators have told me that they deal with this vast range in development by separating the younger middle school students from the older ones in different wings in the building, the house system, or the like. But, these children still ride the school bus together, still have recess together, still use the same restrooms, and still eat in the cafeteria together. In other words, they share the same middle school environment.

Because they share this environment with older more mature teens, your child is going to be faced with many new social challenges in middle school. This is the time when many young people have their first boyfriends and girlfriends. It is the time of the first coed (or what we used to call boy-girl) parties. They may be faced with peer pressure to drink or smoke and even experiment with sexual behaviors.

As I discussed in Chapter Two, they are most likely going through the biggest physical changes of their lives since infancy. These physical changes are usually accompanied by dramatic emotional changes as well. In the words of the National Middle School Association, "young people undergo more rapid and profound personal changes during the years between 10 and 15 than at any other period of their lives." Adapting to middle school can be challenging for both children and their parents.

A high quality school for early adolescents, regardless of its structure, shares certain characteristics, according to the National Middle School Association. As you evaluate your child's middle school, you might want to ask:

- Do the teachers have special training and commitment to working with young adolescents?
- Is there an explicit, shared vision that includes goals for student achievement, student-teacher relationships, and community participation?
- Are there high expectations for teachers, parents, and students?
- Is there one adult advocate for every student as a mentor and guide?
- Are there opportunities for family and community partnerships?
- Is there a commitment to a positive school climate that recognizes that both the physical facilities and human relationships are important to the education of early adolescents?
- Is the curriculum challenging and exploratory?
- Are a variety of teaching and learning approaches used?
- Are there opportunities for student evaluation and not just grades and tests?
- Is the organization flexible to the needs of young adolescents, their diversity, their identification with peer groups, and the need to break out of a rigid schedule?
- Are health and safety important concerns as reflected in policies and programs?
- Are there guidance and support services that provide opportunities for peer discussion, personal attention by professionals, and referrals to specialists when needed?

One of the major changes from elementary school to middle schools for young people is the change in their peer group. As I talked about in Chapter Two, friends become much more important during the early years of adolescence. Not that having friends hasn't been important through your child's growing years, but it is in middle school and the first years of high school that their reliance on their friends and their larger social group reaches a new level of importance.

How Much Pressure Is Peer Pressure?

Despite what many adults think, teens tell researchers that they do not feel that they are pressured directly by their friends to engage in risky behaviors. In fact, it is the reverse. According to a number of studies, teens report more pressure from their friends to *not* drink, *not* do drugs, or *not* have sex than to engage in these behaviors.

Peer pressure—for good and for bad—is only one way that teens influence each other. They also model behaviors for each other, such as what clothes are cool to wear, whether to date, and how hard to work at sports and academics. They set norms for each other of what is acceptable and expected: Is cigarette smoking in or out? Is drinking in or out? Is experimenting with sex in or out? They also can provide opportunities for each other to engage in risky behaviors, such as at unchaperoned parties and houses where parents are not at home.

In middle school, your teen may for the first time feel pressured to engage in certain activities to be part of a group, and for some young people that means smoking, shoplifting, or trying alcohol. Among eighth graders, a surprising 30 percent have a cigarette at least once a day, 13 percent have used marijuana, two-thirds say they have had an alcoholic drink, a quarter say they are current drinkers, and 28 percent say they have been drunk at least once.

Your middle schooler is also part of a teen world that extends far beyond their school and the town you live in.

Television and movies model acceptable teen culture. Take the time this week to watch such teen television shows as *Dawson's Creek, Popular, Malcolm in the Middle,* or *Charmed*. What messages do they give your teen about what it is like to be a teenager today? What clothes and music are presented as cool? How do the teens in these series treat each other? How do they relate to the adults in their lives? What messages do they present about drinking, drugs, and sex? What are the characteristics of the popular characters? The ones that are not? How are the adults portrayed? (One of my biggest complaints about teen-oriented movies and television shows is that the adults are often either stupid or immoral. When Alyssa was in middle school, I sometimes asked her when we watched a show, "Which adults in this show would you like to know?" The answer was usually none!)

Think back for a minute: What were the groups when you were in high school? We had the jocks, the freaks, the in-group, the hoods, and the losers. In today's middle school and high schools, there are the jocks, the preps, the skaters, the populars, the freaks, the nerds, the geeks, the brains, and the metalheads. One of my middle school friends also identifies one group in her school as the "wannabe popular losers." Psychologists call these cliques "reputation-based groups that signal the image or identity adolescents have established among peers." In other words, teens tend to group together in crowds that signal what is acceptable for their dress, attitudes, and behaviors. Movement between these cliques can be difficult: Helping your teen find the right group at the beginning of school may help protect them against risk behaviors.

Teenagers in middle school are likely to have a few close friends and also belong to one of these groups. Most young people in middle school have between one and ten close friends, with the average being about six. Many teens have best friends, although the research says that only one-third of these best friendships last for more than a year. Best friends have a great deal of influence over your child's behavior, but the desired clique may have even more. The research tells us that young people are more likely to change their behaviors to fit into a crowd they would like to belong to than to maintain a current friendship. I remember "losing" several friends in middle school to the more popular, but faster, group as my friends became involved in behaviors that I resisted. The influence of the clique can be very strong.

Interestingly, research demonstrates that the leading crowd in the school, "the populars," may be less influential than your child's immediate circle of friends, despite the fact that pressure to be popular can be intense in middle school. Middle schoolers have a very clear sense of who the most popular kids are and how far away they are from that group. I distinctly remember Alyssa telling me that she was part of the second-most-popular set of girls. The popular group's behavior seems to have no effect, for example, on the timing of first intercourse or the risk of pregnancy. However, there is no question that this leading crowd shapes the norms for the school, for better or worse. For example, in schools where the leading crowd is academically-oriented, mean achievement for all of the school's teens, whether in the leading crowd or not, is higher. In schools where the leading group drinks alcohol, others are likely to follow suit.

Teens in the popular crowd, especially in high school, are more likely to have sexual relationships. This is probably because they are more likely to be invited to parties, date, and have boyfriends or girlfriends than other teens. Conversely, teens who are the most alienated from their peers and school are also more likely to be having sex: Sexual relationships provide a way for them to feel accepted and important.

Hanging out with older friends exposes teens to greater risk-taking behaviors. If your eighth grader is friends with eleventh and twelfth graders, you can expect that they are more likely to be drinking, trying drugs, and experimenting with sexual behaviors than those with friends of the same age. I think it is a good idea to encourage your child to have friends at his or her own grade, or no more than one grade higher. For teen girls, the older her friends are of both genders, the more likely she is to initiate sexual intercourse.

What can a parent do to encourage the right kind of friendships? Here are some suggestions from the National Campaign to Prevent Teen Pregnancy:

- Look beyond your child's best friend to his or her circle of friends and the clique they are in to understand the range of teen influences on your child.
- Know who is in your child's circle of friends. Having lower-risk friends cuts your teen's, especially your daughter's, risk of sexual debut and pregnancy significantly.
- Focus on supporting your teen's relationships with good kids. If your teen hangs out with good role models, they are less likely to engage in risky behaviors themselves. But don't worry about one or two more risky friends, especially if they are of the same gender. Having more "good kids" as friends than risk takers increases the possibility that your teen will also be a "good kid." Most teens are good judges of their friends' behaviors and character and are able to counteract negative influences. By and large, unless given reason not to, trust your teen's ability to make good decisions.

- Be concerned about your child's relationships with high-risk boys and significantly older friends of both genders. Their influence is likely to be negative. Know who your daughter's male friends are; having a close friendship (not dating but friendship) with a low-risk boy seems to be protective; hanging out with high-risk boys actually puts her at greater risk of early sexual involvement.
- Learn about the relationships your child's friends have with *their* parents. Girls who have friends who are close to their own parents are less likely to become involved with sexual behaviors. There is more good news here for parents who are actively involved with their teen's lives: The closer you are to your child, the less dependent they are on their friends for advice and assistance.

One of the biggest challenges for parents of children in middle school is what to do when your child seems to be falling in with the wrong crowd or has a friend you do not like. This may be the last time you can intervene in their choice of friends. Certainly by the time they are in high school and driving, you may not have many ways to provide input into their friendships. But you can now. Just as when your child was younger, you can decide whose house you will let your child visit, who she can go to the mall with, what he can do after school, who she can talk to on the telephone and for how long. But unlike when your child was in elementary school, it is much better to discuss these issues *with* them than to *tell* them what to do. If you are uncomfortable with a particular child or a group of children, invite them over and observe their interaction with you and your child. Trust your instincts; do not be afraid to tell your child that you prefer them not to spend time outside of school with a particular child or group, and tell them why you feel this way. But try to help them reach these conclusions on their own without causing a showdown.

It helps to know your child's friends' parents. These parents can be additional caring adults in your child's life, and knowing them can be helpful in handling peer pressure as well. When Alyssa was in the sixth grade, I grew awfully tired of hearing, "But Jen's mom lets her!" After months of hearing this, I invited Alyssa's five best friends' parents over to our home for cookies and discussion. (Interestingly, only the moms came.) The goal was to see if we could agree to a set of limits about clothes, makeup, and dating for our daughters, goals that we could all share. After all, "But Jen's mom lets her" is much less effective if your son or daughter *knows* that you and Jen's mom share a common set of expectations. And although our family's religious values were very different—we ranged from Unitarian Universalist to nonchurchgoing to Pentecostal—in a few hours, we were able to agree on a set of principles for our seventh graders. This included telephone privileges (calls were limited to ten minutes and there were no phone calls allowed after 8:30 p.m.), makeup (lipstick was okay, eyeliner was not), and dating (we said no). You could also talk about which rated DVDs are acceptable for parties, going to the mall or downtown alone, unsupervised visits at each other's homes, and boy-girl parties.

The day after this type of meeting is an ideal time to talk with your middle school child about peer influences in their lives. Teens need help negotiating among positive and negative influences (these friends want you to drink with them; these friends abstain) and conflicting peer pressure from the media. One of the pressures that many middle school teens report is the pressure to have a boyfriend or girlfriend. This can start as early as the fifth grade.

Going Together

Middle school students do not date; they "go together." And if your middle school starts in fifth grade, you may be surprised to find out that "going together" can begin as early as age 10 or 11.

"Going together" in middle school is not very different than having a boyfriend or girlfriend in junior high school when we were growing up. Young people who are "going together" rarely go anywhere. In one study, less than 60 percent had been to the movies with each other. It still mostly means telling your friend that you like a certain boy or girl, they tell their friend, and if the object of affection consents, a new couple is "born." These couples may wait for each other in the hall, they write each other's names on their notebooks, and they talk on the phone at night. They probably dance only with each other at the school dance or at a party; they may or may not sit with each other in the cafeteria. Sometimes they do not do anything together at all; being known as a couple who "goes together" is enough.

It may surprise you to know that most middle schoolers have been romantically involved with a member of the other sex. Eighty-two percent of 13 and 14 year olds say they have had a boyfriend or girlfriend. In general, these relationships are often very short-lived. It is not unusual at all for them to last only a week or two, and few last longer than three months. Most couples this age do not spend a lot of free time together, and less than half say they are in love.

But, that is not to say that some early adolescents don't experience these early romantic relationships intensely or that parents should simply ignore them. Many adults are condescending about middle school relationships. We even use a condescending term—"puppy love." Indeed, for many middle school students, these relationships are both transient and not terribly intimate. The important thing is *having* a boyfriend or girlfriend—often from the right group—not creating an intimate friendship. It is as if the middle school student is trying on what it is like to be in a romantic relationship. Because most young people this age have not truly developed the capacity for empathy, these relationships can end very abruptly. The same friend who called to find out if you like his friend now calls to tell you that the friend no longer likes you. The relationship is over.

But, for some middle adolescents, these newfound feelings in a relationship can be intense—and the break-ups can be intense too. I can honestly say that the only time in my entire life I have ever considered suicide was when in the seventh or eighth grade, Michael told me that Bobby told him he didn't like me anymore. (Remember that type of situation?) Fortunately, my best friend at the time, Cathy, brought over a gallon of chocolate ice cream, and by the time it was finished I didn't care much anymore. But it could have been much worse. Please see the section on First Love in Chapter Five if your child seems to be having a difficult time dealing with the end of a relationship. Middle school students who are "going together" are also likely to be experimenting with sexual behaviors.

Sex and the Middle School Teen

Even reading this chapter heading may be tough for some parents. What do you mean, sex and the middle school teen? Well, the reality is that some middle school students are engaging in some sexual behaviors. Now, try to relax. That does not mean that most of them are undressing each other, fondling each other, or having sexual intercourse. For most, it means that they are holding hands, kissing, maybe French kissing, and kissing for extended periods of time (what teens still call "making out").

Let's look at the research:

- Seventy-three percent of girls and 66 percent of boys ages 13 and younger have kissed.
- Twenty percent of 13-year-old boys have touched a girl's breasts, and 25 percent of girls this age have had their breasts touched.
- Twenty-three percent of boys and 18 percent of girls ages 13 and younger have fondled someone's genitals.

These behaviors can be thrilling...and frightening. Think back for a moment to the first time you deeply kissed someone of the opposite sex. Not during spin the bottle or another party game, but someone you really liked and cared about. Can you remember who it was? Where you were? What you thought? How about putting your arm around someone or having someone put their arm around you? Holding hands together? Slow dancing?

Boy, do I remember slow dancing in the seventh and eighth grade. I think I still know all the words to *Cherish* and *As Tears Go By*, staples at our parties in parents' basements. And although I didn't have the vocabulary to describe it then, I remember being both taken by and scared of how my body reacted to being held so closely, barely moving to the music from the record player. I also remember being both amazed and a little frightened by the boys' erections that I felt against my leg, and wondering if this happened to other girls. I was never brave enough to ask back then, but I do remember that after it had happened several times, I secretly felt thrilled by how powerful it was to have boys reacting to me this way.

At that age, I had no vocabulary to understand what was happening. I didn't know about French kissing, until the first time my eighth-grade boyfriend put his tongue in my mouth. I bit him! I didn't know about erections or why my underpants would get wet while I was slow dancing with a boy I liked. And I grew up in a home where we talked about sex!

It can be very helpful to your child to talk about these issues. It can also be pretty difficult for both of you. It can help to share your own early adolescent sexual experiences with kissing, French kissing, and slow dancing with your child. You can use the situations in movies or television shows to talk about how the characters are making decisions about these issues. If your child is in a pretty serious "going together" relationship, you will want to talk to them about sexual limits. See Chapter Four for more information about setting sexual limits.

Recently there have been several newspaper articles about students in middle school engaging in oral sex. The first story appeared in the *Washington Post* and was about a group of eighth graders in Virginia who were reportedly in an oral sex club. Other stories have appeared in other parts of the country. The reports had a distinct gender bias: Girls were reported to be performing fellatio; boys were not offering cunnilingus to their girlfriends. The reporters (and the parents) were outraged. I did several television interviews about this so-called oral sex trend.

The good news for parents is that this trend may be a media invention. Think back for a minute: When you were in the eighth grade, did you know a girl or a few girls who were the "bad girls" who were supposed to be sexually experienced? I did—in fact, I can even remember their names. (I'll spare you—and them!) I believe that there are indeed some middle school teens who are engaging in pretty sophisticated sexual behaviors, but most teens this age are not. However, we have no research on oral sex in middle school—not from when we were teens, not now. Politics simply keeps researchers from being able to ask these questions. What we can surmise is that as a result of the news about the Clinton scandal, some young people may be trying oral sex earlier than we did.

However, we do have research on the number of young people in middle schools who have tried sexual intercourse, and the good news is that few young people have ever done so. Only 6 percent of teens had their first sexual intercourse below the age of 13. The percentage of the youngest girls having intercourse has decreased as well; in 1995, one in five girls under age 15 had had sexual intercourse; now fewer than one in six have. But studies indicate that many girls who report intercourse before high school were coerced into the sexual experience or even sexually abused. More than a quarter of teens under the age of 15 who have had sexual intercourse say that their first intercourse was involuntary. Yet these girls are also more likely to have subsequent voluntary sexual relationships, and they are less likely than other girls to use contraception in future sexual relationships.

I think almost all parents and all professionals will agree that middle school students are too young to be having sexual intercourse of any kind, whether it is penile-vaginal or oral sex. They simply do not have the emotional maturity to be engaging in these types of sexual behaviors. What the research tells us is that most of the young people this age who are engaging in such advanced sexual behaviors are troubled kids. They are not having their need for feeling connected, powerful, or loved met by their parents, schools, and communities. They may be living in communities that seem to have abandoned them; in one study of an inner-city area, half of the boys had had intercourse by age 12.5. Early adolescents may use their bodies and their sexuality to meet their normal adolescent needs for love and affection. If you discover that your middle school teen is having intercourse or oral sex, it may be time to seek professional mental health counseling or at least an evaluation. These young sexual adventurers may be struggling with self-esteem issues; there may be family issues that need to be addressed.

Parents sometimes ask me how it is possible for middle school teens to be engaging in sexual behavior at all. After all, they do not have cars or credit cards for motel rooms. What teens tell us is that sex is happening most frequently at parties—and after school, when their parents aren't home, often in their own or their parents' bedroom.

Boy-Girl Parties and School Dances

In many middle schools, coed parties become popular. When I was growing up, these were called boy-girl parties, and I still remember that my mother wouldn't let me go to the one that my friend Sherry had the year we were 11. In many communities, these invitations start coming as early as the fifth grade. Indeed, some middle schools sponsor dances for the fifth and sixth graders, and by seventh grade, dances are common events. Many parents are concerned that their 10- and 11-year-old children just are not ready for the pressures of these parties and dances.

For the most part, these parties are harmless rehearsal for later adult social interactions. Boys often go and hang out with their friends on one side of the room, girls on the other. The first time I chaperoned a middle school dance, I was both amused and a little disconcerted to see how little had changed in thirty years. The girls still waited for the boys to cross the gymnasium to ask them to dance; shy teens didn't dance at all.

Alyssa and her friends at the end of the night counted how many times they had been asked to dance by how many boys, just like I had in the 1960s. The only difference I could see was that the teens wore blue jeans where we had been in dresses and the boys in navy blazers with ties.

I think it is a good idea to talk with your child about their expectations prior to the dance or the party. Encourage them to be outgoing and dance in groups or with anyone who asks them (at least once). Help them think through how to politely turn down someone who they don't want to dance with more than once. (The one-dance suggestion really can help avoid some crushed adolescent feelings, but more than once in the world of middle school may imply a commitment!) Encourage your daughter to dance with her girl friends and to ask boys to dance. Encourage your sons to ask a number of girls to dance, not just the ones they think are special.

You, of course, want to make sure that these parties and dances are safe places for your child. Call and make sure that the school dance is going to have chaperones or consider volunteering to be one. (Alyssa only let me chaperone once; she said, "Mom, I don't want my friends ending up in your books!") Call the parents who are holding the party and make sure that they are going to be there. Know the time the party or dance begins and the time you need to be there to pick your child up.

Make sure you feel comfortable with the parents' concepts of what it means to be a good chaperone at a private house party. Staying upstairs all evening while the party is downstairs in the basement is not enough. I do recommend that parents appear in the party room at least every half hour or so to bring more food, tidy up, and let the kids know that you are there.

Just like thirty years ago, boy-girl parties in parent's basements are still the scenes of kissing games. Yes, early adolescents are still playing "spin the bottle" and "pass the grape-fruit." They also play "suck and blow," a game with a name that is much more suggestive than it is. It involves passing a playing card around from one person's mouth to another. In "Lemon," strips of paper are marked "kiss," "lick," or "touch" and the names of body parts. Youth are to follow the directions of the strips of paper they pick. In "Wild Kiss," a boy and a girl wrestle each other to give or avoid giving each other a kiss. "Truth or Dare" is very popular among teens. "Truth" is answering an embarrassing question. "Dare" generally involves telling some-one to kiss so-and-so, but sometimes the suggestions are more sophisticated.

I basically think these types of games are harmless, and within reason, I think that parents do not need to break them up. Kissing games give young people a chance to kiss someone without the pressures of "going together" and satisfy a bit of curiosity. However, by popping in now and then you help assure that they don't proceed into other activities. Parents should have an absolute rule that bedrooms are strictly off-limits at parties.

However, even middle schools parties can get out of hand. In the stories I have read about the "oral sex clubs" I talked about earlier, the scene is almost always a party where parents weren't home. Now, it is hard for me to imagine how a parent allows a 12 or 13 year old to have an unsupervised party (or even be away long enough for it to happen), but it does occur. Make sure you speak to the parent of the child who is hosting the party, no matter how well you know the child.

Before we leave middle school parties, let me share with you my bias about another new trend I've heard about. In some parts of the country, parents are holding coed sleepovers for middle school children. That's right, boys and girls are both invited to spend the night. Indeed, some youth groups hold lock-ins, a more chaperoned version of a coed sleepover held in a church social hall or community organization auditorium.

Frankly, I'm not sure what the adults are thinking who arrange such events. These parties send young people very mixed messages: On the positive side, they say that it is good to be friends with both boys and girls and that we trust you. On the negative side, they give these concrete thinking, peer-pressure-prone middle schoolers more opportunity for sexual exploration than is wise. In the intimacy of a darkened room in pajamas and sleeping bags, what happens when one girl says, "I've always wanted to see a real penis" or "What if we all kissed each other good night with our tongues?" In the words of child expert Barbara Meltz, "What may start out as the preteen equivalent of playing doctor could turn into something with far more serious consequences." Rumors about what happened at the party can fly, and teens who don't participate may feel pressure to exaggerate their own behavior. If your church or youth group is planning to hold such a lock-in, make sure you know that the boys and girls will actually sleep in separate rooms and that there is an awake adult chaperone in each room with adult monitors in the halls between the rooms.

Of course, parties are not the only places where middle school teens can get into trouble. Young people are spending increasing amounts of hours unsupervised—most often, in their own homes.

Unsupervised Time

Middle school often poses a new challenge for parents. School ends at 2:30, there is no after-school program, and you don't get home from work until 6:00 p.m. Millions of children between the ages of 10 and 12 are latchkey children: They come home from school and are unsupervised for several hours a day. The good news for parents is that most studies have found that early adolescents do fine in self-care: They do as well in school, have similar reports of self-esteem, and demonstrate the same levels of social skills as children with parents at home after school. However, more to the point of this book, some studies suggest that the more time middle school students spend alone in their homes, the greater the likelihood that they will experiment with alcohol and sex.

The current wisdom is that children should not come home from school alone until about age 12, but some are ready at about age 10. According to the Canadian Child and Family Department, you need to assess your child's readiness for self-care. They suggest that you ask yourself:

- Does she want to be on her own?
- Is she afraid to be alone in the house?
- Can you depend on him to follow house rules when you aren't there?
- Can you rely on her to tell the truth?
- Does he have common sense?
- Can she deal with unexpected situations in a positive way?
- Can he amuse himself or does he need constant supervision?

If the answer to any of these questions is "No," your child is probably not ready to be home alone.

Experts recommend that you "latchkey-proof" your home just like you baby-proofed your home when your child was younger. This includes making sure that the doors have deadbolts; that your child knows how to use the fire extinguisher (and that you have one in working order!); that you have smoke detectors on every floor of your house (with batteries that work!); that there is a first aid kit; that emergency numbers are posted and that you have agreed upon emergency procedures; that alcohol is locked away; and that there is emergency money placed in a safe spot.

There are some basic guidelines for middle school children who are home alone after school. You want to make sure that your child knows that you are still involved and available even if you aren't there at 3 p.m. Try leaving little love notes or funny notes for your child to find. It is a good idea to ask your children to check in with you as soon as they arrive home. By checking in with your child at a specified time each day, you make sure they have gotten home, ask about their day, and you can remind them to do their homework, chores, and practice. You can also tell them that you love them, how terrific you think they are, and other similar expressions of love and affirmation. Make sure your child knows an adult to contact in the neighborhood if she needs help, thinks the house may have been broken into, or is followed home. And, of course, review procedures for contacting the police or 911. When you do get home, make sure you spend time with your middle schooler to talk about their day and show you are interested in them. Put aside making dinner for a while or ask them to help you so that you let them know they are your first priority.

As I talked about in Chapter One, you can also do your best to involve your child in after-school activities. Not only does this help with cutting down unsupervised time, but it also helps your child feel connected to the larger community. Sports, clubs, music lessons, church groups, youth groups, and volunteer activities all offer important opportunities for your middle school child. And as I noted in Chapter One, being involved in activities both in and out of school cuts down the risk that your early adolescent will start drinking, smoking, and having sex.

I think you need to have strict limits on visitors in your home when you are not there. You may feel comfortable having your child's best friend over when you are not home. In fact, that may be a good way to help increase your child's comfort level with being in the house alone. But one child—probably of the same sex—who you know and trust should be the limit. You absolutely want to be sure that your home will not become the place that kids congregate after school because they all know that no adult is present. A home with a liquor cabinet and bedrooms is just too tempting for middle school students who have difficulty setting limits and anticipating consequences. Allowing your middle schooler to entertain their boyfriend or girlfriend in your home (or allowing them to spend unchaperoned time at the other's home) is asking for trouble. Be sure you also clarify whether your child can go over to someone else's home, and if so, be sure you have a system where they contact you for permission so that you are not frantic when you call and find no one home.

One of the benefits latchkey children report is that they feel more responsible than other children their age. They also have ample opportunity for privacy and time alone. This gives them opportunities for daydreaming, writing in their journals, and even time to explore their sexuality alone.

"How Come He's in the Bathroom Again?"

There are some topics that are difficult to bring up with your children, no matter how open you have been previously, and no matter how old they are. Masturbation is one of these.

In fact, many married couples have never had a frank discussion about masturbation with each other. I like Woody Allen's definition of masturbation in the movie *Annie Hall.* He said something like masturbation is sex with the person you love the most—and who will never turn you down!

During the early adolescent years, after the onset of puberty, many boys and girls begin to masturbate for sexual pleasure. Research tells us that about three-quarters of boys and about half of girls under the age of 15 masturbate. This is different than children's casual genital touching. Teens at this age, just like adults, are seeking pleasure and orgasm. Masturbation is usually the first way that teens—and indeed some adults—experience orgasm and ejaculation. (By the way, ejaculation and orgasm are not always simultaneous for men, and ejaculation can occur without orgasm.)

Some boys seem to "take up" masturbating during puberty. Parents of adolescent boys in particular often call me concerned about the amount of time their son seems to be locked in the bathroom or their bedroom. Both the boys and girls I have taught in middle school want to know more about masturbation. They ask questions like: How much is too much? Is it normal not to masturbate? Can masturbation cause physical harm?

Here are some basic facts about masturbation your early adolescent needs to know:

- Many boys and girls masturbate for sexual pleasure during puberty, but some never masturbate at all.
- It is normal to masturbate and it is normal not to.
- Masturbation does not cause physical or mental harm.
- Most people have masturbated at some point during their lives.

They need to know that how often a person masturbates varies for every individual. I like to teach middle school students what my colleague Sol Gordon taught me. He tells people that the answer to "How much is too much?" is "Once is enough, if you don't like it." If masturbating seems to be interfering with your child's school, homework, friends, or your family life, it is too often. Otherwise, frequency is highly individual. Some adults masturbate more than once daily; others once a year or never.

You do need to decide if there are limits you want to put on your child's behavior. If there is only one bathroom in the house or your child shares a bedroom, be sure to talk to them about finding times where they can be alone without inconveniencing others.

Many sexologists think that learning about one's body through masturbation is important for adult sexual functioning. By masturbating, teens are learning what feels good to them and how to experience sexual pleasure. Equally important, teens need to know that if kissing and touching a partner arouses them, they can come home and masturbate to orgasm later when they are alone. Indeed, in one study, teen girls who masturbated regularly to orgasm were less likely to have intercourse than girls who did not, and more likely to report orgasm when they did have sex with a partner. Some adults have told me that they wish they had known to tell their teen partners to go home and masturbate instead of becoming involved in intercourse as teenagers. I heard Cybill Shepard say on a talk show that she wished as a teenager she'd known about masturbation, not motels! Of course, this is also controversial. In the 1990s, U.S. Surgeon General Jocelyn Elders lost her job when she suggested that masturbation be taught as part of HIV/AIDS prevention. Some families oppose masturbation on religious grounds, and if you feel that way, you will want to share that value with your early adolescent. But know that forbidding the behavior is unlikely to stop it, although it will probably make your child feel guilty and ashamed. Regardless of your beliefs, every child needs to know that masturbation will not cause them physical or mental harm.

Many early adolescents first feel the desire to masturbate as they look at erotic pictures—either in magazines, Victoria's Secret catalogs, or on the Internet.

Erotica and the Middle School Child

Okay, you are thinking, now she's gone too far. Erotica and the middle school child? Well, like it or not, the fact is that your early adolescent is likely to have viewed sexually explicit materials in magazines, on M-TV and VH1, on the Internet, and in PG-13 and R-rated movies. This is certainly one of the changes since we were growing up. Many of my adult male friends report using *National Geographic* to see women's breasts or the Sunday *New York Times Magazine* for pictures of women in their underwear. Gay friends of mine tell me about sneaking peeks at books in the public library. My husband remembers his friends passing around sexually explicit 8-mm films and holding them up to the light.

The reality today is that young people have much easier access to sexually explicit materials than we did, and it may be more graphic. The Victoria's Secret catalogs alone show hundreds of pages of beautiful women in tiny underwear that do not leave much to the imagination. Early and middle adolescent boys in particular may be thrilled to look at *Playboy* and *Hustler* magazines or online sex sites.

Many parents of middle school boys have called me for

advice after they have found sexually explicit materials under their child's mattress while they are changing the sheets, sex sites in their child's Internet histories, or sexually suggestive text messages. Although I can't quote any statistics about how common this is, it seems to be pretty frequent, especially among adolescent boys. Thinking through in advance can help you be prepared for how to handle this if it does happen to you. Like other "oh no, what do I do now" situations, whether you react calmly or with anger and shock is much more likely to influence your child than what you actually say.

Think about your family values about sexually explicit materials. Americans profess a dislike for sexually explicit materials, but more than one in five adults used them in the past year. More than 600 million X-rated videos are rented each year, and the commercial sex sites are making the most money of any e-commerce venture on the Internet. Adults are clearly seeking these materials.

Parents often want to know whether seeing erotica will hurt their child. There is no research showing that exposure to sexually explicit materials harms teenagers. It may simply be a response to their developing curiosity about sex. Remind yourself that this curiosity is perfectly normal. In a class I taught a few years ago, every eighth-grade boy checked on a questionnaire that he wanted to see pictures of naked women; half of them said they already had.

So, what do you do if you find erotica in your child's room or find that your child is looking at sex sites? You could choose to ignore it and put it back where you found it. But, then you would be missing a teachable moment to talk about your values. How do you feel about the way sexuality is portrayed? Are you comfortable with your son or daughter looking at them? At having such materials viewed in your home? You have a right to set limits on the types of materials you allow in your home, and you can certainly require that they be kept out of view. You should set limits on Internet use. You can also make sure that your middle schooler has some of the books listed in the resources section that have explicit drawings to respond to their curiosity about what men and women really look like or how people have sex.

It's Time to Leave the Baby Doctor's Office

Your middle school child still needs an annual physical and still needs to have a series of immunizations. In fact, most states require 12-year-olds to have an immunization against Hepatitis B, a blood-borne sexually transmitted disease. According to the American Medical Association, your child needs a thorough physical exam once between 11 and 14 years of age; once between 15 and 17; and once between 18 and 21. They should be screened for high blood pressure; nutritional habits; alcohol, tobacco, and drug use; emotional issues; school issues; and their involvement with sexual behaviors. Young people who have had intercourse of any kind should be screened for sexually transmitted diseases, and sexually active teen girls should have an annual PAP smear. (Otherwise, a girl can wait until she is 18 or 19 for her first PAP.) Girls between 9 and 26 can now be immunized against cervical cancer.

You are likely to find that your adolescent is reluctant to sit in the waiting room of the pediatrician's office, with its building blocks and copies of *Highlights* magazine. Enter the physician (who may be a pediatrician or an internist) or nurse practitioner trained in adolescent medicine. These health care providers are generally pediatricians who have advanced training in taking care of the special needs of adolescents. They generally specialize in treating young people ages 12 to 21. They are skilled not just in the physical problems of adolescents but also in understanding their emotional growth and development.

Unfortunately, there are fewer than 500 board-certified adolescent medicine specialists in the United States. A major teaching hospital may have a special teen program. Or a large group practice may have a physician with a practice that is primarily for adolescents. For a list of certified adolescent medicine providers, visit the website of the Society for Adolescent Medicine (www.adolescenthealth.org) or contact them at 1916 NW Copper Oaks Circle, Blue Springs, Missouri 64015, (816) 224-8010. If there is not an adolescent medicine specialist in your area, consider switching your teen to an internist or family physician with an interest and commitment to serving teens.

When Alyssa was entering the ninth grade, an adolescent medicine clinic finally opened at one of our area hospitals. I was delighted to take her for a visit at the clinic. We both participated in filling out her medical history, and then Dr. Schneider saw her alone. At the end of their forty-five-minute visit together, we all met together to discuss a few issues. I was happy and relieved that Alyssa now had her own doctor, someone whom she could confide in and seek out for questions that she might not feel comfortable asking me.

The next day, however, I understood how really great this was. I was driving Alyssa and one of her girlfriends to the movies. Lisa was complaining that she had to go see her old pediatrician for her school physical and how much she hated visiting the "baby doctor." Alyssa told her that she was now seeing an adolescent medicine doctor who only took care of teenagers. She then said, "She answered questions I didn't even know I had." I knew then that I had definitely made the right choice.

Special Issue

"How Old Were You When You First Had Sex, Mom?"

As I traveled during the book tour of *From Diapers to Dating*, one of the questions I was most frequently asked was, "How do I handle questions about my personal sexual history?" Parents have told me that they have been asked when they first had sex, how many people they've had sex with, whether they have or have had oral or anal sex, and even whether they have had an affair. Baby boomers seemed particularly troubled by questions about their sexual and drug histories. As *Boston Globe* columnist Ellen Goodman once wrote, "Baby boomers did everything, regret nothing, and want their children to do none of it." A colleague of mine, Dr. Victor Strasburger, titled his now-out-of-print book *Getting Your Kids to Say No in the 90s When You Said Yes in the 60s.*

Middle school teenagers often want to know about their parents' lives when they were growing up. They love to hear stories about you when you were young and how you handled tough situations. I encourage you to share your memories of middle school and the problems you faced with your teenager. This type of sharing helps build trust between you and provides a "teachable moment" to talk about your values for their behaviors.

Middle school teens might also be asking these types of questions to get under your skin or test your limits. They may, of course, be genuinely curious about your sexual history. Most likely though, I think they are seeking to find out more about sexuality and how to make good decisions. They are also providing you with a teachable, if not uncomfortable, moment.

I do not think parents have to share the details of their sexual experiences with their children. It is okay to tell your child that there are parts of your life that you choose to keep private. (Know also that there may be parts of their lives that they will choose to keep private from you.)

You need to think through how you will respond to your teenager's questions about your personal sexual history and experiences. Partly this will depend on whether your experiences as a teen support the values you want to share with your teen. Let me explain. If you believe that teens should not have intercourse until college, and you were in college when you first had sex, your experience supports those values. You could say, "I was in college when I first had sex. I hope you will wait until then too." On the other hand, if you were 13 and you hope that they will wait until they are 18, telling them the truth may undermine your message. If that is the case, you can say something like, "I'm not comfortable sharing this type of personal information with you at this point. But, it sounds like you are wondering how people decide if they are ready to have sexual intercourse. In our family, we think..." and then give your values. Talk about how people might know if they are ready or not ready for a mature sexual relationship.

You also might be willing to share with your child how you have made important choices in your life. In a SIECUS booklet titled "Now What Do I Do?" psychologist Bob Selverstone suggests that you could say, "I'm happy to talk about my choices. I gave them a lot of thought, and they were right for me at the time. My choice may not be the right one for you when you get older. But first, tell me why you want to know." This communicates that wise choices require thought, that some decisions are right for some people at certain times and not for others, and that parents can help their children choose wisely.

Your child may ask about your current sexual behaviors. "Do you and daddy _____?" I do not think that in most cases it is appropriate to share the details of our current sex lives with our children. You can say to your middle schooler, "What daddy and I do is our private business. It sounds though like you are curious about what sexual behaviors adults engage in. We can talk more about that if you would like." Most psychologists would agree that you should never talk to your child about an extramarital relationship.

Parents who are single and dating face other issues here. Their children may ask them questions about their current sexual behavior with the people they are dating. Remember, actions do speak louder than words. Try to be honest with your middle school child about your feelings, but it is not appropriate to make them your confidant. You also need to carefully think through bringing sexual partners into your home when your child is around. Your dating behavior is definitely setting a model for your child's future dating. If you do not want your teen having sex in your home with a string of lovers, you do not want them to see you doing this either. If you are seriously involved with someone and want your partner to share your bed in your home, be sure to talk to your children about it first. Do not let them discover you! Share your behavior in a way that is consistent with the values you want to set for them. You could say something like, "Ellen and I have been seeing each other for half a year. We love each other a great deal. As adults, we want to share that love together in our home. We are beginning to think that we would like to share private time together in our home. I'd like her to stay over in my room. How would you feel about that?"

This simple exchange does several things. You have told them that love and sex go together, that this is an adult decision, and that you care about their feelings about what goes on in your home. You have let them know that you are willing to talk about sexuality without going into the details of your private adult sexual behavior.

Values Exercise for Chapter Four

Your ninth-grade daughter comes home and tells you that she is going to the junior prom with a boy you haven't met. You:

   ❏ a) Say, "How exciting for you. Let's go shopping."

   ❏ b) Say, "You're too young to go out with a junior. You can't go."

   ❏ c) Ask her to invite him for dinner so you can check him out for yourself.

   ❏ d) Tell her you need to discuss this later after you've had a chance to talk with your spouse or partner about it.

Your tenth-grade son comes home from a school dance smelling of alcohol. You:

   ❏ a) Ground him for a month.

   ❏ b) Ignore it; after all, boys will be boys.

   ❏ c) Wait until morning and then ask him what happened the night before.

   ❏ d) Give him a lecture about the evils of alcohol.

You walk into your den and see your 15-year-old daughter in the arms of her boyfriend without a shirt on. You:

   ❏ a) Turn around and leave quietly, muttering "sorry."

   ❏ b) Freak out, and yell, "Get dressed immediately."

   ❏ c) Calmly ask them to meet you in the living room for a discussion.

   ❏ d) Ground your daughter.

You think teenage sexual experimentation is:

   ❏ a) A natural and healthy part of growing up.

   ❏ b) To be avoided at all costs; teens should not do more than lightly kiss.

   ❏ c) Scary when it is my child you are talking about.

   ❏ d) Okay, as long as it doesn't go too far.

Chapter 4
Starting High School
Ninth and Tenth Grades

Starting High School

I'm willing to bet that you can remember your first day of high school. I can see myself at fifteen in my purple miniskirt and purple print blouse. I remember feeling incredibly nervous: Would I fit in? Would I find my locker? Would I find my classes? Would I make friends with the kids from the other junior high school? Would I find a boyfriend?

Fast forward nearly thirty years, and I am watching Alyssa get ready for her first day of high school. Unbelievably, she is going to the same high school that I did, as we moved back to my hometown several years ago to be closer to my family. No skirt for her, she worries about which jeans and top to wear. But otherwise, her concerns echoed mine from 1969.

Being in ninth grade is tough. Ninth graders are the youngest students in the school; they still need to be driven to school by their parents or take the bus; they need rides for after school activities. They leave the safety of being on top at middle school, and they have to start over, often in a bigger and unfamiliar school.

What does starting high school have to do with sexual health? Well, it is in high school that most young people in America begin seriously experimenting with sexual behaviors. It is in high school that they are likely to fall in love for the first time. It is in high school that they are likely to begin to have a stronger sense of their own sexual orientation. And it is in high school that they are likely be exposed for the first time to unchaperoned parties, peer pressure to drink and try drugs, and media images that tell them that all teens their age are "doing it."

Mom and dad, expect that you, too, will be faced with new parenting challenges as your child enters high school. It will be harder to know your child's teachers. It will be harder to know your child's friends, and even harder to know the parents of your child's friends. Your 14- or 15-year-old is likely to become less communicative, even if you have had open communication up until now. He or she is also going to be a lot busier with after school, evening, and weekend activities. It is going to be tougher to monitor those activities. And watching your child's sexuality develop and blossom is likely to raise a lot of feelings and concerns.

Talking to your soon-to-be ninth grader before school starts about whether they are excited, scared, or a bit of both helps let them know that you are still there for them. Sharing your own memories of starting high school may help remind them that you were a teenager once too. Sharing your expectations for their behaviors lays the groundwork for future discussions. Sharing your expectations for their sexual behavior may make the difference between a teen who starts having sexual intercourse in the early years of high school and one who waits.

Sexual Behavior: What to Expect

Most ninth and tenth graders are just beginning to engage in romantic relationships, which includes beginning experimentation with sexual behaviors. In most communities in the United States, teenagers in the early years of high school are not dating, but "going together." The norm in early high school is partnering with one boy or one girl, and not spending Friday night with one person and Saturday night with another. Frankly, I'm sorry about this. I have very fond memories of dating a lot of boys in high school, and I think it was important rehearsal for adult relationships. It also gave me the opportunity to learn about different types of boys. Because it wasn't serious, I could go on dates with jocks, academic types, and less popular boys. I remember my attitude was that any boy could take me to the movies once.

In today's high schools, if a boy or a girl asks you out, they are asking you to "go together," not just to spend a single evening together. This is usually before any real conversation with the person and certainly before a friendship is established. The criteria, teens tell me, include things like whether the person is cute, popular, well built (or "buff" in teen slang), and whether they seem nice. In other words, the decision to go out is mostly based on physical attraction and popularity. No wonder these relationships often do not last more than a few weeks. High school couples actually begin to go places together: to the movies, concerts, school dances, the mall, and to parties.

If your child is "going together" with someone, expect that they are engaged in kissing and French kissing. Most teens aged 15 and 16 say that dating couples their age kiss (93 percent) and French kiss (71 percent), and just under half (48 percent) say they also engage in petting. Unlike their younger brothers and sisters in middle school, they actually do "go out" some place: Sophomores say that couples their age go on dates and spend a lot of their free time together. More than half say that couples their age are in love with each other. In other words, many teens in the ninth and tenth grade are experiencing their first feelings of love and their first feelings of adultlike erotic arousal, including erections for boys and lubrication for girls.

There is so much your teen needs to know about these feelings, and who better than a parent to prepare them? Yet, few parents talk about sexual pleasure with their teen children, or for that matter, good sexual decision making. It is critical that your ninth and tenth grader, particularly if they have a boyfriend or girlfriend, knows that it is one thing to have a sexual feeling and it is something else to act on it. Holding hands, kissing, French kissing, and stroking can be intensely arousing to teens this age; they need to know that they can enjoy these feelings and not go any further sexually. Boys need to know that "blue balls" are an overstated problem: They can have an erection for hours, without orgasm, and they will not suffer any negative health effects. (And they can be told that masturbation easily takes care of their sexual tension after they bring their dates home!)

Most ninth and tenth graders stop at French kissing and fondling, but among a significant minority of ninth- and tenth-grade virgins, there is significant involvement in fairly advanced sexual behaviors. For example, one-quarter of ninth-grade virgins and one-third of tenth-grade virgins have been masturbated by a partner and have masturbated a partner. Seven percent of ninth graders and 12 percent of tenth graders have experience with fellatio that includes ejaculation (and no doubt percentages are higher where ejaculation did not occur), and similar percentages have experience with cunnilingus. One percent reports that they have had anal intercourse at least once.

A significant minority of young people has sexual inter-course (penile-vaginal intercourse) in the ninth and tenth grades. Nearly four in ten ninth graders (38 percent total: 41 percent of the boys and 34 percent of the girls) report that they have had sexual intercourse. By the tenth grade, slightly more than forty percent (42.5 percent) have had sexual intercourse, with girls now exceeding boys in sexual experience (43.5 percent compared to 41.7 percent respectively.) Even more sur-prising, 12 percent of the ninth graders and 13.8 percent of the tenth graders report that they have already had four or more sex partners in their lifetime. Still, even among teens who have a history of sexual intercourse, sexual activity is sporadic. More than a third of teens this age who have had intercourse haven't done so in the past three months.

Condom use is remarkably high among the ninth and tenth graders who are having sexual intercourse, although use of the more effective contraceptive methods is still very low. Nearly 60 percent (59.2 percent of the boys and 58.3 percent of the girls) in the ninth grade who have had intercourse used a con-dom at last intercourse. However, only 8 percent used the birth control pill. In fact, the younger the teenager, the less likely they are to use one of the more reliable contraceptive methods.

Many of the younger teens who are having sexual behaviors report that they use alcohol and drugs before they have sex. Nearly four in ten boys and more than a quarter of girls who had intercourse in the ninth grade report alcohol and drug use at last intercourse. These numbers drop consistently during the high school years, so that by senior year, only 17 percent of girls and 28 percent of boys used alcohol and drugs at last inter-course.

The good news here? Well, parents can make a big difference in helping their teen choose abstinence during these early years of high school. Almost every professional I know, and certainly the vast majority of parents, think that the fact that one in four ninth graders have had intercourse is shocking. I cannot think of any parent who would be happy to know that their middle school child is having sexual intercourse. You can help your teen learn to set sexual limits.

Helping Your Teen Set Sexual Limits

Let's face it, when was the last time you negotiated sexual limits with a sexual partner? If you are married or partnered, over time, you have probably just "learned" what is acceptable to your partner. If you are single and dating, how do you talk to a new or potential partner about how far you are willing to go sexually? How do you introduce these topics?

Or, like many adults do you just get started and wait to see what happens? Think for a moment about television and movies. For the most part, in the media, new couples engage in lustful kissing, and move quickly into bed. When was the last time you saw two adults on a television show or in a movie actually discuss that they would like to kiss and touch but not move to other sexual behaviors or that they would like to enjoy nonpenetrative sexual behaviors but wait to have intercourse?

I bring this up because adults are not modeling how to communicate about decisions about sexual behaviors with our teenagers. Most parents have not talked to their teens about setting sexual limits, and schools are unlikely to be teaching teens much beyond "just say no."

Despite their pseudo-sophistication talking about sexuality, teenagers today are still using a code that dates at least back to when I was a teenager: The boys' job is to try to move to the next steps sexually, and the girls' job is to set limits, all without the benefit of any discussion. In one focus group study, one of the boys summed up the male rules this way: "The gods are going to have to forgive me, because I am going to test the waters." In one study, the authors concluded, "Teens seemed more fearful of embarrassment talking about sex with a partner than they were fearful of STD and pregnancy."

But unless teens learn to communicate, the results may be disastrous. Not only is it difficult, if not impossible, to negotiate condom and contraceptive use without at least some talking, but also without clear consent, boys may find themselves accused of sexual assault. When I've asked teen boys how they know the girl is giving her consent, they often say something like, "You just know." When I ask girls if they sometimes say no, but mean maybe or yes, they nod their heads. It is not surprising than that more than three-quarters of teens say that their first intercourse was unplanned or just happened.

I told Alyssa that I never want her to tell me that her first experience with sexual intercourse just happened. I remember what my own mother told me, "You will always remember the first time; make sure it is special." (You do, right? Almost all adults can recall the story of the first time they had intercourse; unfortunately, many of both my women and men friends recall it was not a very pleasant or romantic experience, and many report that they had not planned for it or used a contraceptive method.) It is no surprise than that a majority of teens who have had sexual intercourse wish that they had been older when it first happened.

Regardless of your values about teenage sexual intercourse, your teenager needs skills to know how to set sexual limits with their boyfriend or girlfriend. Some teens decide they will go no further than "making out"; others decide that they will only have intercourse if they are in love and if they are using a contraceptive method. How can we as parents help them know their limits and stick to them?

Well (and at this point in the book this isn't going to surprise you) you need to talk with your teen about this. Start by sharing your values about teenage sexual expression, and then talk to your teen about how they will communicate their decisions about sexual limits to their partner. Let them know that they have the ability to stick with their decisions. Sexual feelings in the moment should never overrule a previously made decision. If your teen is feeling he or she would like to go further than they and their partner have agreed to in the past, ask them to take the time to think more about this at a later point and not just move ahead that moment. You may want to help them role-play how to talk with their boyfriend or girlfriend about sexual limit setting. They could practice by saying, "I really like you and I've enjoyed our sexual experiences so far, but I'm not prepared to go farther than _____. I want to know that you will respect that boundary until we talk about this again."

Do you remember the bases in high school? When I went to school, first base was necking, second base was a boy touching a girl's breast, third base was genital touching, and home base was sexual intercourse. Today's teens name the bases much more crudely: They talk about the four "F's": frenching, feeling, fingering, and well, you know the fourth "F."

According to the research, teens move faster today through these stages of intimacy than we did thirty years ago. Many tell me that if they are going to do more than kiss, they will probably have intercourse. Oral sex is seen by some as a way to engage in sexual intimacy or to "hook up" with losing their virginity.

It is also incorrectly viewed as "safe." Some teens have told me that they have oral sex instead of penile-vaginal intercourse because it doesn't have risks for pregnancy and sexually transmitted diseases. Only half true. Only a few of the teens I have met during the past years know this. Recent studies by the Centers for Disease Control and Prevention have found that almost 8 percent of people who became infected with HIV in the past year were infected through oral sex. Oral sex can also transmit herpes, chlamydia, gonorrhea, and trichomoniasis. Your teen needs to know that fellatio needs to be performed with a condom and cunnilingus with a dental dam, a small piece of latex covering the vulva. They also need to know that they cannot swallow ejaculate or have oral sex during menstruation. If these topics seem too embarrassing to discuss, consider how awkward it would be helping your teen with oral gonorrhea or, worse, HIV.

Teenagers often ask me, "How do I know if I'm ready for intercourse?" Of course, if your value is no intercourse until marriage, you can answer your child, "When you get married." But many parents do not share that value, and most parents themselves did not wait until marriage to have intercourse. Many of my friends who are sex therapists believe it is actually a bad idea to not have a sexual relationship before marriage, as both the chemistry, the vulnerability of a sexual relationship, and sharing of passion is such an important part of most marriages.

While I was at SIECUS, I helped develop a list of the criteria for a moral, sexual relationship. We said that a moral sexual relationship has five characteristics. The relationship should be:

- Consensual
- Non-exploitative
- Honest
- Mutually pleasurable
- Protected against sexually transmitted disease, and pregnancy if penile-vaginal intercourse occurs

Let's see how this works. Think for a minute about what we knew about the relationship between former President Bill Clinton and Monica Lewinsky. Consensual? Yes. Non-exploitative? Hardly. Honest? No. Mutually Pleasurable? Not according to the President. Protected? Not according to the stains on the dress! (Even oral sex has a degree of risk for STD and HIV transmission. Penises need to be covered with condoms during fellatio and dental dams or thin pieces of latex should cover the clitoris and vaginal opening during cunnilingus when the HIV status of the partner isn't known.) The semen stain on the dress is a pretty good indication that a condom hadn't been used!

These are pretty rigorous standards, which apply equally to 16 year olds and 55 year olds, regardless of marital status. They apply whether one is straight or gay. I believe that if we taught teens to evaluate their relationships based on these criteria, fewer of them would have sexual intercourse or other intimacies that lead to emotional or physical risk. Frankly, I believe they would help adults, married and single, as well.

Teenagers a few years ago in one of my classes came up with a mnemonic to remember these criteria. (You remember mnemonics . . . "Every Good Boy Does Fine" is the way to remember the notes on a scale.) This mnemonic is "Can U Have My Pleasure?" C is for consensual; U is for using; H is for honest; M is for mutually pleasurable; and P is for protected. If your teenager cannot answer yes to all of them, suggest to them that they are not ready for a mature sexual relationship that includes any type of intercourse. And there is no way that they can know that all of the criteria are present unless they are communicating with their partner.

The National Commission on Adolescent Sexual Health came up with a list of characteristics for a teenager who is ready to engage in a mature sexual relationship. They said that each individual in the relationship needed to be:

- physically mature;
- patient and understanding;
- knowledgeable about sexuality and sexual response;
- empathetic and able to be vulnerable;
- committed to preventing unintended pregnancies and STDs; and
- able to handle the responsibility of both positive and negative consequences; and honestly approving of their own behavior.

In addition:

- the relationship between the two individuals should be committed, mutually kind, and understanding;
- the partners need to trust and admire each other;
- the partners should have experimented and found pleasure together in non-penetrative behaviors;
- the partners must talk about sexual behaviors before they occur;
- the partners must have a place to have sex that is safe and comfortable; and
- the motivation for the sexual relationship should be pleasure and intimacy.

A pretty daunting checklist for most 15- or 16-year-olds—actually it might be a hard list for the adults who are reading this!

An important part of helping your teen set sexual limits is limiting the amount of privacy your teen can have for sexual exploration. Teens tell researchers that they have sexual intercourse in two places—in the boy's parents' bedroom when no one is home and at parties. Indeed, it is unchaperoned parties that are the scenes of most teenage casual sex.

Parties

The middle school boy-girl party seems almost sweet compared to what happens at high school house parties. It seems that every weekend someone is throwing a party at their parents' house. These parties no longer involve kissing games; they often involve alcohol, drugs, and sex. One teenager I interviewed said to me, "Debra, parents would never let us go to parties if they knew what went on."

Your ninth or tenth grader may ask you to hold a party at your home. Hosting a party for a group of teenagers can be both fun and just a little bit scary. Remember, you are legally responsible for anything that may happen to a minor who has consumed alcohol or drugs at your home. In order to limit sexual behaviors at your home, and also drug and alcohol use, you need to develop an agreement with your child about which behaviors are okay and which are off limits. Let them know you will be actively chaperoning the party, and consider inviting some other adult friends to help you. Active chaperoning means being present in the home; coming into the party rooms periodically and unannounced with food, to clean up, etc.; and taking action if you need to. For example, if a young person arrives at your home for a party and has clearly been drinking, do not hesitate to call their parents to pick him or her up.

Here are some party "rules" to discuss with your child:

- No alcohol, drugs, or smoking.
- No uninvited guests. (Go over the guest list with your child in advance. Tell them you will turn away uninvited guests so they do not have to.)
- Lights will be left on.
- The party will be limited to certain rooms. Bedrooms are off limits.

Some parents do not believe that they need to actively chaperone teen's parties. After all, aren't teens old enough to be responsible for their own behavior? When teens were asked in a series of focus groups where high-risk sexual behavior was most likely to occur, the most common answer was a party where the parents weren't home. Teens volunteered that at these parties, alcohol and other drugs are common, judgment becomes impaired, and peer pressure to "hook up" can be intense. One-night stands become common.

I think it is also important, if you are going to be away for evenings or weekends, that you talk explicitly with your high-school-age child about your rules for guests when you are not home. As an adult, you are still legally responsible for what happens in your home even if you aren't there. There are a remarkable number of unchaperoned parties going on; do not be naïve enough to believe that it could not happen in your home. Make sure your child knows that you know that such parties happen, and that it would be unacceptable for them to have a party while you are away. Several of my friends have had the experience of finding out in advance that a teen party was planned for their home and then having their sons lie to them. In one case, a friend cancelled her trip. In another, the parents arranged for an adult house sitter to stay over.

What about when your child is going to a party? Well, this is not going to make me very popular, but I think it is essential to call and talk to the parents of the teen who is hosting the party. Alyssa cringed when I did this; she asked me to stop when she was in eleventh grade. It was the reason for some of our biggest disagreements after she entered high school. I think you will be surprised by how often parents plan not to be home or say that they will be entertaining adults upstairs while the teens are downstairs. Remember it is your job to keep your child safe. Call the parents and find out if they are planning to be home all evening to supervise. (And if they were not, I would not let my child go. You will have to decide, but a house full of unsupervised 14, 15, and 16 year olds with a liquor cabinet, VCR, and bedrooms is a teen pregnancy waiting to happen!) Ask parents what their rules are for the party.

If you decide to allow your teen to go, make sure you have an agreement with them. Role-play with them an easy way to leave the party if they feel it is not a safe place. Ask them to anticipate your concerns about the party, and then to tell you how they will respond if they do arise. Be sure they have a ride home. Be sure they know what their curfew is. And I think it's a good idea to try to wait up for them when they do get home to check in on how it went.

One of the reasons unchaperoned parties in early high school become so problematic is that they are often the scenes of alcohol and drug use.

Alcohol and Drugs

Nationally, most teens drink socially at least once in the first years of high school. Just about every teenager in their first years of high school will have to make a decision about whether or not to drink or use illegal drugs. Look how common drinking is: More than seven in ten ninth grade boys and girls have had had a drink, and almost half of boys in the ninth and tenth grades have had five or more drinks in the past thirty days. Almost half of teens in high school report having tried marijuana, with one in four using it in the past thirty days.

Teens who drink are far more likely to become involved in sexual behaviors. Teens aged 14 and younger who drink are twice as likely to have sex as teens who don't drink, and young teen drug users are four times more likely to have intercourse. One-fourth of sexually experienced high school youth said that they had used alcohol or drugs the last time they had sexual intercourse. (It is not clear which starts first, sexual intercourse or drinking or drug use. It may be that teens who drink are also more likely to engage in other high-risk behaviors like having sex, or it may be that teens have sex because they are drinking.)

Many parents assume it is safe to let teens drink in their homes as long as no one is driving. But here are some facts from Students Against Destructive Decisions that you should know:

- It is illegal everywhere in the United States for anyone under the age of 21 to drink alcohol.
- It is a crime to sell or give alcohol to anyone under 21— even your own children.
- If you host a party in your home where alcohol is served to ten of your teen's friends and you are caught, the fine could exceed $23,000 and a year in jail.

SADD encourages parents to tell their teen children that they will not tolerate the use of alcohol and drugs, and to assure them that you will know if they have been drinking or doing drugs. They encourage parents to talk to their teens about how to refuse alcohol, other drugs, or a ride with someone who has been drinking "without looking like a wimp." They encourage parents and teens to work out a plan if they are in a dangerous situation and need adult help.

One would think that designated-driver campaigns, which have been around since I was a teenager, would be enough. But significant numbers of teens report drinking and driving or driving with someone under the influence. One-third of boys in the tenth grade and nearly one-third of the girls said that, in the previous month, they had been in a car with a driver who had been drinking alcohol. Personally, these statistics scare me more than the ones on sex: Driving under the influence kills thousands of teenagers and their passengers each year. Be sure your teen knows that you will always give them a ride—no questions asked—if their driver has been drinking.

The data on parental involvement in curtailing drinking and drug use is very encouraging. Teens who have close relationships with *both* parents are far less likely to be involved with substance use. A significant number of teens say that they have not gotten drunk or tried marijuana because of discussions they have had with their parents. Just like with sexuality, parents' opinions really do matter. And it seems that here, too, moms are doing more talking than dads: Teens say that their relationship is better with mom, that she is easier to talk to about drugs, and that they are more likely to go to her when faced with decisions about substance use. But in homes where both mom and dad are involved, teens are even less likely to drink and do drugs. The bottom line message:

Talk to your teens and tell them you do not want them to drink or do drugs.

Telling your children you will know whether they have been using alcohol and drugs is one thing. Knowing the danger signs is another. Your child doesn't have to come home acting drunk with slurred speech or unsteady gait for them to have been drinking. According to Students Against Destructive Decisions, "Be aware of any changes that take place in your child, however subtle. Each drug has different effects." A partial list of signs to watch for includes:

- Bloodshot eyes, dilated pupils, wearing sunglasses indoors
- Insomnia
- Loss of appetite
- Increased alertness
- Slurred speech
- Disorientation
- Euphoria
- Drowsiness
- Nausea
- Constricted pupils
- Hallucinations
- Relaxed inhibitions
- Increased appetite
- Headaches
- Fainting
- Change in friends
- Change in study habits
- Declining grades
- Loss of interest
- Increasing anger, hostility, irritability, secretiveness
- Stealing

- Depression
- Rebelliousness against set rules and regulations
- Argumentativeness
- Increased unwillingness to discuss opposing ideas or feelings
- Isolation

Of course, some of these "symptoms" are characteristics of many early and middle adolescents. The important thing is to watch for sudden changes in your child's behavior. If you suspect alcohol use, talk to your child. If you have serious reasons to believe that your child is taking drugs, confront them with your suspicions. If they deny it and you are still concerned, I think this is one of the few reasons to violate your teen's privacy and search their room and their belongings. Better to be proven wrong and deal with those consequences than have a teenage child who overdoses and dies.

Date Rape Drugs

Drugs and alcohol existed when we were teenagers, but today there are new drugs for parents to be concerned about. These date rape drugs are also one of the best reasons I know that parties need to be carefully chaperoned. In 1998, 15-year-old high school freshman Samantha Reid went to a party with two girlfriends, instead of to the movies as she had told her mother. While there, a group of boys put a mixture known as GHB into the girls' glasses of soda; within minutes of sipping the soda, she collapsed. A few hours later, she died in an emergency room. One of her friends went into a coma for a half a day but recovered. The other girl did not touch her drink. On March 14, 2000, the three teen boys, ages 18 and

19, were found guilty of involuntary manslaughter. They each face up to fifteen years in prison. The boys told the police that they had put the GHB in the girls' drinks to make the party more "lively."

GHB stands for gamma hydroxybutyrate. It is colorless and odorless. It can be made in a kitchen using ordinary household products. The recipe can be found on the Internet. The myth is that the drug will cause girls to want to have sexual intercourse, but then will not remember that they did it. The truth is that it can produce a temporary feeling of euphoria, hallucinations, and temporary memory loss. The truth is that it can also cause someone to become unconscious, stop breathing, and die. The truth is that there have been sixty-five deaths due to GHB since 1990, more than 5,700 cases of documented GHB abuse, and more than thirty sexual assaults reported to the Drug Enforcement Administration. The primary victims are teenage and college-age young women. The secondary victims are the boys who do not know that what they are doing is wrong, illegal, and potentially life threatening.

Rohypnol is the other most common date rape drug. It is also known as "roofies" and "roach." Rohypnol is not legal in the United States, but is used in more than sixty other countries to treat insomnia. It is available in small white tablets that can be taken orally, ground up in drinks, or snorted. It leaves its users feeling intoxicated, and it can cause deep sedation, respiratory distress, and blackouts that can last up to twenty-four hours. It can cause overdoses and even death, especially if mixed with alcohol.

What's a parent to do? First, talk to your teen about GHB and other date rape drugs. Ask your teen if they have heard of them. It is sad, but your teen needs to know that they can't leave open soda cans around at parties. They should keep the cans with them, take them along to the bathroom, or start a fresh can if they leave it anywhere. I can hear Alyssa saying, "But mom, no one I know would do that." This is one case where it is certainly better to be cautious even if it seems silly. Here are other suggestions from SHOP TALK, a newsletter from the Sexuality Information and Education Council of the United States:

- Drink only from tamper-proof bottles and cans, and insist on opening the bottles yourself.
- Do not drink from group drinks such as punch bowls.
- Insist on pouring or watching while any drink is mixed or prepared.
- If you think you have been drugged, do not be afraid to seek medical attention.

Your teen should know, and you as a hosting parent should know that if a teen becomes unconscious at your home, suspect GHB or Rohypnol and call an ambulance right away. Immediate medical attention by someone who knows that date rape drugs are a possibility can make the difference between life and death.

Date rape drugs have received very little coverage by the media. I have yet to see a teen-oriented television show cover this issue. But, one of the major ways that teens learn about relationships and sexuality is through the media. It teaches them about romantic relationships, sexual relationships, and how to be sexually attractive.

The Media

Teenagers consume a huge amount of media. In fact, young people from pre-adolescence through high school spend an average of 6.5 hours a day using both electronic and print media—not including any used in school or for homework. According to the Kaiser Family Foundation, the average American child grows up in a home with 3.5 television sets, 3.6 CD players or tape recorders, 3 radios, 2.9 video/DVD players, 2.1 video game players, and 1.5 computers. Increasingly teens control their own media: More than 70 percent have a radio in their bedrooms, two-thirds have a CD player, and nearly two-thirds of young people ages 8 to 18 have their own television set in their bedroom. Three-quarters of teen girls grades seven through twelve regularly read "teen magazines"; more than four in ten boys these ages read sports magazines.

It is not your imagination that media, especially television, has gotten much more sexually explicit than when we were young. It wasn't until 1964 that a married couple shared a bed on television (*Make Room for Daddy*) or that a woman was able to show her navel (Yvette Mimieux in a *Dr. Kildare* episode.) In 1978, television saw its first teen lose his virginity (*James at 16*). It wasn't until 1987 that we saw a teen use a condom (*The Hogan Family*). Masturbation was not mentioned until 1992 (*Seinfeld*).

Today, sexual messages, sexual innuendo, and suggested sexual acts pervade the media. More than half of evening programming on television includes sexual content; these shows average more than five scenes about sex per hour. Seventy percent of all network prime-time shows include talk about sex or sexual behavior, averaging more than five incidents per hour. In one study of the most popular teen shows, the characters talked about sex or engaged in sexual behavior in at least two-thirds of the episodes. Yet, only one in eleven programs mentioned anything to do with pregnancy or STD prevention or the consequences of unprotected sex.

Teens learn a great deal about sexuality from the media. More than half of high school boys and girls say they have learned about birth control, contraception, or pregnancy prevention from television. Almost two-thirds of the girls and 40 percent of the boys said they had learned about these topics in a magazine. One ninth-grade girl recently told me that she was very disappointed that *Gilmore Girls* has gone off the air. "Debra," she said, "I learned so much from this show, about AIDS, relationships, eating disorders, love, and alcoholism."

Many parents are concerned that television portrays a very limited range of sexual relationships. Often, sex is only for the young, attractive, and single, and sexual relationships are almost always highly romantic, spontaneous, and risk free. The message to teens is often that everyone their age is doing it. (And for those of us married adults, the message is often perceived as everyone else is having hotter, better, and more frequent sex than we are!)

What's a parent to do? First, I think it is important to know the media your child is consuming. Make it a point this week to pick up one of your teen's magazines. Are they reading *Teen People? Seventeen? Men's Fitness?* What are the messages about sexuality in these magazines? Turn to the cable television stations MTV or VH1 and watch music videos for an hour. If you haven't done this recently, you may be surprised by how sexual (and how violent) some of the videos are. Between one-fifth and one-half of music videos are explicitly sexual or erotic. Ask to see their Web page and the Web pages of their closest friends.

Second, consider limiting the media your teen has access to

in the privacy of their bedroom. Cable television and computers with unfiltered Internet access in particular can expose your child to a wide range of images that they (and you!) may not be ready for!

Third, try to share some of this media time with your child. I was surprised to read that 95 percent of children over 7 say that they usually watch television alone. I believe strongly that children under 12 should almost never be watching prime-time television alone; there are just too many incidents of sex, violence, and other adult themes that need interpretation. But even a ninth or tenth grader can benefit by watching programs with his parents. Ask your child what his favorite television programs are, and ask if you can watch this week's episodes together.

It can be easier to talk with your teens about what is happening on the screen than what is happening in their very own lives. Here is some advice I've adapted on how to use television as a teachable moment with your teenager from The Media Project in Los Angeles, California.

- Watch with them without offering your opinions at first. Sit back, relax, and just watch. Wait for the commercials to talk.
- Ask your teen's opinion. Ask what they or their friends might do in a similar situation.
- Share your thoughts and opinions about what you see happening. Share your values about what you hope your son or daughter might do in this situation.
- Use keys to good communication. Remember you are seeking a dialog, not a chance to lecture your teen.

You will also want to have a discussion with your ninth

and tenth grader about your expectations about their going to R-rated movies. The movie rating system is G (general audience), PG (parental guidance suggested), PG-13 (parents strongly cautioned), R (restricted under 17, requires accompanying parent or adult guardian), and X (adults only). The reality is most middle school teens are watching PG-13 movies, and most high school teens think they are ready to see R-rated movies, despite being under the age limit. The irony is that many of today's R-rated movies are designed pretty explicitly for teenagers. The recent films *Knocked Up* and *Superbad* could only be categorized as teen movies; both carry R ratings.

As a result of congressional concern, movie theaters have tried to be stricter about access to R-rated movies by teens. The telephone taped message for our local Cineplex states that all patrons for R-rated movies must be 17 or older, must show photo ID if they are under 25, or must be accompanied by a parent or adult guardian. Further, the tape warns, parents must actually accompany their minor in the theater; if they are found watching different movies, they will both be asked to leave.

That is the policy. In reality, every teen I know 15 and older has managed to go into an R-rated movie alone in our town. The multiplexes make it pretty easy; buy a ticket to a PG-13 movie, wait until the usher is not looking, and enter the R-rated door.

What's a parent to do? Well, the best advice I can give you is to do what the rating system says: Go with your teen to these movies. Greg and I have a deal. He can see any R-rated movie he wants as long as he goes with me and he agrees to a half-hour of discussion afterward about anything I think needs to be explained. I agree to keep my mouth shut during the movie. It gives me a chance to see more teen movies than I might otherwise, and it provides a ready-made teachable moment.

R-rated movies, however, are tame compared to what your teen may be finding on the Internet.

The Internet

More than three-quarters of homes have Internet access. In a typical day, just about half of preteens and teenagers will use a computer. According to a recent study, one in three young people ages 10 to 17 encountered unwanted pornography in the past year on the Web, and one in seven has received an unwanted sexual approach online.

Surfing is a wonderful way for teens to obtain information on an unimaginable number of topics. It is helpful for school, research, playing games, and seeing new places. It is also the easiest way for people of any age to access sexually explicit materials.

As an experiment when I first wrote this book, I typed in "sex sites" at the AOL search engine and at Yahoo. I found almost 21,000 matches at AOL. Here's some of what came up on my screen at AOL first: one hundred sex sites; a hardcore sex site; a lesbian sex site; and, unbelievably, www.teenagesex.com, a site of pictures of naked teenage girls. One click got me to pictures of women kissing each other and a woman performing fellatio, all before I was asked for credit card information. At Yahoo, I turned up sixty-nine sex sites, freexxxsexsites, four free sex sites, and 2ezfind, all promising free pictures at the next click. These sites do warn that you need to be 18 to keep clicking; I just find it hard to believe that is going to be much of a deterrent to a 15-year-old boy or girl.

Teenagers are actually more likely to get in trouble on the Internet than younger children, according to Lawrence J. Magid. He says, "Teens are more likely to explore out-of-the-way nooks and crannies of cyberspace, they're more likely to reach out to people outside of their immediate peer group, and sadly, they're more often preyed upon as victims of pedophiles and other exploiters." A couple of years ago, I read an article in the *New York Times* about Internet pedophilia. In one year, nine men in Westchester County, New York, had been convicted of or pleaded guilty to sexually abusing boys as young as 13 who they met on the Internet. The defendants, according to the *Times*, were a Yonkers city official, a former member of the Somers school board, a former chairman of the New Castle planning board, and a retired spokesperson for PepsiCo Inc.

The article included an account of a troubled 15-year-old boy who had become a regular in a chat room for men to arrange sex with other men. The boy is described as "struggling in school, socially unpopular, and questioning his own sexuality." His profile said that he liked older men, and all nine of the convicted men met him in person. His mom said he spent all his free time on the computer, even bringing his laptop on family vacations.

I think it is important that you have an agreement about online safety with your children, including your teen children. Teenagers need to know that people online may not be who they say they are; a person with a teen profile could actually be an adult pedophile. The National Center for Missing and Exploited Children suggests that you have rules, which might include:

- I will keep my personal identity private. I will not give out personal information such as my full name, address, telephone number, parent's work address or telephone number, or the name and location of my school without my parent's permission.

- I will tell my parents right away if I come across any information that makes me feel uncomfortable.
- I will never agree to meet someone offline without first checking with my parents. I will never meet someone offline by myself. I will always bring someone and the meetings will only be in a public place, like a coffee shop or mall that I know well. The safest procedure is to have my parents talk with the parents of the other person first and for both of us to bring our parents to the first meeting.
- I will never send a person my picture or anything else without first checking it out with my parents.
- I will not respond to any messages that are hostile, belligerent, inappropriate, or in any way make me feel uncomfortable. It is not my fault if I get a message like that. If I do, I will tell my parents right way so that we can contact the online service.
- I will talk with my parents so that we can set up rules for going online. We will decide upon the time of day that I can be online, the length of time I can be online, and the appropriate areas for me to visit. I will not access other areas or break these rules without first checking with my parents.

They also suggest that teens, especially girls, use gender-neutral names in chat rooms, not names like hotchick or sexy-grl that I saw in a recent visit to Facebook. They suggest that teens be asked to not respond to spam mail or e-mail from someone they don't know.

Parents, you need to learn everything you can about the

Internet and social networking sites. Let your teenager teach you. Have them show you great places for teens and places they think you would enjoy. Ask to see their Web page. Use the Internet together to plan your family vacation or pick out activities.

Encourage your teen to come to you if they encounter a problem online. This is where setting the foundation for talking about sexual issues will come in handy. If they tell you about something, don't blame them or take away their Internet privileges. Work with them on how to avoid problems. Know that how you respond to the first problem will partly determine if they come to you the next time they have a problem.

I do not think that filters are a good idea for adolescents. These services or commercial products rate websites for content and block sites that someone deems inappropriate. The problem is that they often block good information, and in some cases, block your teen's ability to surf the Internet completely. For example, many of the filters block out access to the American Cancer Society because it provides information on breast and testicular exams, and others block out all feminist, gay and lesbian, and sexual information sites.

There are better non-electronic ways to protect children on the Internet. My best advice is do not put a computer with Internet access or wireless in your child's bedroom where you have no idea what they are looking at. Keeping the computer in the living room, family room, or den means that all use is observable. An involved parent is much better protection than a computer-based baby sitter. The website SafeKids.com provides up-to-date information on keeping children safe online.

Some teens—just like adults—may get in trouble on the Internet. They spend way too much time on shopping, gambling, games, or sex sites. Monitor your child's Internet use. Set limits of an hour or two a day. If your child has trouble keeping to these limits or is sneaking time, talk to them. If it seems out of control, seek professional help.

About one in six teens report that they have received unsolicited sexual advances or upsetting e-mail comments while they are online. But do not think that limiting your teen's access to the Internet will keep them free of such harassment. Every day, your teen may be facing such unwanted sexual advances and hearing sexual put-downs at school.

Dealing with Sexual Harassment in Schools

Has your teenager ever talked to you about being sexually harassed at school? No? Ask them tonight whether they have ever been touched sexually in a way that felt uncomfortable or put down by a harassing comment. And then ask them if they have ever done the same to someone else.

I was frankly surprised—and appalled—by the prevalence of sexual harassment in middle and senior high schools. Eighty-five percent of girls and 76 percent of boys in grades eight to eleven say that they have been the targets of sexual harassment. Sixty-six percent of these teenage boys and 52 percent of the girls admit they have sexually harassed someone. The average teen is both a victim and a perpetrator of sexual harassment. Education researcher Valerie Lee says that schools have a "culture of harassment"; teenage girls in particular cite harassment and bullying as one of the most difficult parts of their lives.

The most overt sexual harassment is when a school employee lets a student know that she or he must submit to unwelcome sexual conduct in order to participate in a school program or activity, or that an education decision such as a grade depends on sexual conduct. This is legally known as "quid pro quo harassment," and it is illegal. Here is what one student wrote to the advice columnist Beth Winship:

"Dear Beth: I'm 18 and in high school. I have this really cute math teacher.... One day he asked me to a fancy restaurant to talk about my grades. He just kept telling me how beautiful I was and asked if I could come over to his house next week...he told me it would bring up my grades. I get very bad grades in math...what should I do?"

In addition to quid pro quo, sexual harassment also includes a hostile school environment. This occurs, according to the Department of Education, "when unwelcome sexually harassing conduct is so severe, persistent, or pervasive that it affects a student's ability to participate in or benefit from an education program or activity, or creates an intimidating, threatening or abusive educational environment. A hostile environment can be created by a school employee, another student, or even someone visiting the school, such as a student or employee from another school." *Unwanted* sexual conduct that constitutes harassment includes repeated sexual advances; touching of a sexual nature; graffiti of a sexual nature; sexually offensive gestures; sexual or dirty jokes; pressure for sexual favors; touching oneself sexually or talking about one's sexual activity in front of others; and spreading rumors about or rating other students as to sexual activity or performance.

Sexual harassment sometimes takes the form of hazing. In a town near where I live, eight members of the wrestling team were suspended for hazing three freshman members of the team. The hazing included locking the boys for a half hour several times in their gymnasium lockers and reportedly inserting plastic knives into their rectums.

Girls as young as 12 and 13 report being called "bitches," "sluts," and "whores" and being asked crudely at school for sexual favors. One in four high school girls say that they regularly hear such insults. Here is what one girl said in a focus group: "Someone said that I was a slut. You always try to pretend that what people say about you doesn't affect you, but it does. You slowly start to believe what's being said about you." In an article in the *Washington Post*, a middle school girl reports that she is daily asked at school, "When are you going to give me head?"

Touching, rubbing, and physical harassment is also not uncommon. One girl said, "There were two or three boys touching me…and I'd tell them to stop but they wouldn't. This went on for months. Finally I was in one of my classes when all of them came back and backed me into a corner and started touching me all over…after the class, I told the principal, and he and the boys had a little talk. And after the talk was up, the boys came out laughing because they got no punishment."

Well, they should have, because such behavior is *illegal*. A United States Supreme Court decision in May 1999 found that schools may be held financially liable for such harassment, even if it is between two students.

What's a parent to do? First, talk to your teenager, both your sons and daughters, about these issues. Find out what is going on in their school and whether this behavior is frequent. Ask them if they have ever been the victims of sexual harassment. Talk to them about how to respond assertively to any unwanted behaviors or language. They can learn to say, "Get lost," "Stop this now," or "If this happens again, I will report you." Let them know you will help them deal with such a situation if it gets out of hand and that you hope they will come to you. It is also important that your teens understand that it is unacceptable to treat others this way.

But this is not just a matter of teaching your child assertiveness skills. Find out if your teen's high school has a specific sexual harassment policy. If not, suggest to the administration that it be developed. According to the U.S. Department of Education, the best way for a school to deal with sexual harassment is to prevent it from occurring. They suggest that all schools:

- Develop and publicize a sexual harassment policy clearly stating that sexual harassment will not be tolerated and explaining what types of conduct will be considered sexual harassment.
- Develop and publicize a specific grievance procedure for resolving complaints of sexual harassment.
- Develop methods to inform new administrators, teachers, guidance counselors, staff, and students of the school's sexual harassment policy and grievance procedures.
- Conduct periodic sexual harassment awareness training workshops for students, administrators, teachers, and guidance counselors.
- Establish discussion groups for both male and female students where students can talk about what sexual harassment is and how to respond to it in the school setting.
- Survey students to find out about the sexual harassment occurring at the school.
- Conduct periodical workshops for parents on sexual harassment.

Talk to your teen about what to do if he or she is being sexually harassed. Ask them to come to you. The behavior should then be reported as soon as possible to a responsible school official. This could be a teacher, principal, faculty member, guidance counselor, or the school's Title IX coordinator. Let them know that you expect action to be taken to stop the harassment. Let them know that you will both pursue legal action and contact the Office of Civil Rights at the U.S. Department of Education if the harassment is not addressed.

Special Issue

Preventing Eating Disorders

Anorexia and bulimia do not just happen to other people's children. Concern about weight and looks are ever present in high schools. Almost four in ten high school students say they have been on a diet in the past month. In 2005 more than 5 percent of high school girls took laxatives or vomited to lose weight or to keep from gaining weight. Six percent of girls took diet pills. By college, one out of every four women is believed to have an eating disorder.

It is not just young women who have eating disorders: As many as one million teen boys are believed to have an eating disorder. Two percent of teen boys have vomited or taken laxatives and more than 2 percent have taken diet pills. About 5 to 10 percent of teens with anorexia are boys. More and more young men are becoming preoccupied with working out as well as dangerous practices like steroid use. Four percent of boys have used illegal steroids (without a doctor's prescription) to help them build their bodies.

It is very hard in contemporary American culture for most people to feel good about their bodies. In a survey of 2,000 teenage girls, *Seventeen* magazine found that 46 percent said that they were unhappy with their bodies, and 35 percent would consider plastic surgery. The Body Shop has a slogan that says, "There are three billion women who don't look like supermodels and only eight who do." A study done in 1995 of adult women found that three minutes spent looking at models in a fashion magazine caused seven in ten women to feel depressed, guilty, or shameful. And models are getting thinner: Twenty years ago, they weighed 8 percent less than the average woman; today they weigh 23 percent less. Male models are also getting thinner: The ideal now is a washboard six-pack set of abdominals, something that is only possible if one has less than 20 percent body fat. Given our cultural preoccupation with thinness, it shouldn't come as a surprise that the number-one wish of a majority of teen girls is to lose weight.

This cultural obsession with thinness is peculiarly American. A few years ago, in a workshop in Venezuela, I asked a group of health professionals, "True or False, I like my body just the way it is." When I ask that question in the U.S., less than one in six people raise their hand. In Venezuela, every person in the room did. Now, they did not *look* any better than a similar group of adolescent health professionals in the U.S.; they just lived more comfortably in their bodies and understood that it is health, not thinness, that is important.

Of interest, in the United States, African-Americans tend to have much better body image than Caucasian Americans. African-American teenagers want to be heavier than white teens and report higher levels of body satisfaction. Their attitudes about weight reflect the adults in their lives as well: African-American adults report greater satisfaction with their bodies compared to white adults, despite on average being heavier and more prone to being overweight.

Helping your teen develop a positive body image begins well before the teenage years. But it is particularly important to talk about these issues during this stage of adolescence.

Remember these are the years when teens have an "imaginary audience": They think that everyone is looking at them. According to the Eating Disorders Awareness and Prevention Program, having a positive body image includes:

- A clear, true perception of one's own body.
- Celebrating and appreciating one's own natural body shape.
- Understanding that physical appearance says very little about one's character or worth.
- Feeling proud and accepting of one's own unique body.
- Refusing to spend an unreasonable amount of time worrying about food, weight, and calories.
- Exercising for the joy of feeling one's body move and grow stronger.

Young people with negative body image are more likely to suffer from low self-esteem and more likely to be depressed.

Okay, mom and dad, be honest...how do you feel about your body? What are the messages you are giving to your teenager? Do you meet the criteria listed above as having positive body image?

So often, the parents who have talked to me about their concern about their child being too thin or anorexic are modeling unhealthy images about weight. I remember this one woman vividly: a size two, beautifully and expensively dressed, middle-aged but incredibly toned, she anxiously said to me, "I'm worried that my daughter cares too much about her looks and her weight." Well, duh, as Alyssa would say. When we are constantly dieting, constantly working out, and constantly talking about our weight, we are telling our children that they too should be consumed with how they look. When we try to regulate our children's food consumption, diet, or exercise, we are going even further: We may be creating the foundation for eating disorders.

Here are some things parents can do to encourage a positive body image:

Teach teens the importance of eating nutritious well-balanced foods and the value of moderate exercise. Do not categorize food as "good/safe" or "bad/dangerous."

Talk about healthy eating. Each day, your teen needs three to five servings of vegetables; two to four servings of fruit; six to eleven servings of breads, cereals, rice, or pasta; three or more servings of milk, yogurt, and cheese; and two to three servings of protein. In addition, teens need iron in their daily diet: 12 milligrams a day for boys to sustain their rapidly growing body mass and 15 milligrams a day for girls to offset losses due to menstruation.

Do not regulate your child's eating. Don't make comments about how much they are eating. (I have actually watched a friend take a second piece of bread out of her 13-year-old daughter's hand. Do not do this; it only encourages your child to hide food from you for bingeing later.)

Look at your own attitudes about thinness and weight loss. If your child is heavy or overweight, it does not mean that you are a bad parent or that your children are lazy or bad. Remind your children and yourself that a person's weight or body shape tells nothing about a person's character or value. Be sure you are not inadvertently giving your child messages that you will love them more if they are thin or that they will feel like a better person after they lose weight.

Help your child be a critical viewer of media portrayals of perfect bodies. Talk about the images on television and in magazines, especially advertisements. Remind your teens (and yourself!) that the models in the magazines are made up by professionals, airbrushed, and touched up. I think I once read that Cindy Crawford said, "Even I don't look like Cindy Crawford in real life."

Educate yourself and your teen about the genetic basis of differences in body shape and weight. Be sure that they understand that weight gain is normal and necessary during the early years of adolescence. Remind them that if they have inherited Grandma Anna's heavy calves, all the exercise and dieting in the world will not change them. And then remind them that it really does not matter.

Encourage your teen to get regular physical exercise and to enjoy what their bodies can do and feel like. Work with the school to see that your child has a range of physical education opportunities to pick between; as a teenager, I remember being tyrannized by having to play field hockey, a game that I just could not master. Remember that fitness and size are not the same.

Avoid negative statements about your own body and eating. If you are constantly complaining about your own body, know that your child is likely to become critical of his or her body as well.

Avoid making weight and eating a control issue between you and your teen. Make sure they eat something for breakfast, lunch and dinner, but allow them to decide portion control. Have healthy snacks available. Ask them what they would like you to have in the refrigerator and the cupboards. Have them come shopping with you and ask them to help plan meals.

It is also critical that you become aware of the early symptoms of anorexia nervosa, bulimia nervosa, and binge eating disorder. Parents can help recognize eating disorders before they spin out of control.

Anorexia most often appears in early and middle

adolescence. Some of the signs of anorexia nervosa are abnormal weight loss of 25 percent or more, with no known medical illness; sharp reduction of food intake; denial of hunger; elimination of carbohydrates and foods with fats; prolonged exercising despite fatigue and weakness; and intense fear of gaining weight.

In contrast, people with bulimia appear to eat normally and remain within a normal weight range. They often binge in private, rapidly consuming extremely high-calorie foods followed by self-induced vomiting or other forms of purging. Bulimics are usually older than young people with anorexia; it seems to begin in late adolescence, and some researchers estimate that as many as 20 to 30 percent of college-age women may have some bulimic behaviors. Signs of bulimia include consumption of extremely large quantities of food with high caloric content, alternating with periods of fasting; self-deprecating thoughts; and depression. Unfortunately, it is more difficult to detect bulimia, as the person will usually try to hide their vomiting, laxative, or diuretic use.

Binge eaters are similar to bulimics, except that they do not fast, vomit, or purge. They eat huge quantities of high-caloric food in single sessions repeatedly. This is not the teen boy who can finish off a carton of milk, but the teen who can eat an entire gallon of ice cream with fudge sauce and whipped cream in one evening. Unlike bulimics, binge eaters are usually severely overweight; they may appear to eat normal portions at dinner but continue to gain weight.

If any of these signs occur or persist, consult your child's physician or a specialist in eating disorders. Do not wait for your teen to come to you for help. In one study, six in ten girls with symptoms of eating disorders told researchers that they did not need counseling. The reality is that eating disorders can be fatal; as many as 5 to 15 percent of young people with an eating disorder will die from it. Eating disorders can also cause chronic kidney problems, irregular heartbeats, stomach and intestinal problems, parotid gland swelling under the jaw line, and dental problems. You need to take charge and seek help for your son or daughter. The list of organizations in the last chapter can help.

Values Exercise for Chapter Five

First sexual intercourse should take place in:
- ❑ a) A committed, caring relationship.
- ❑ b) Marriage.
- ❑ c) College—let them at least get through high school.
- ❑ d) The junior year in high school.

You find a packet of condoms in your son or daughter's room while you are putting away clean laundry. You:
- ❑ a) Do and say nothing. After all, you respect their privacy, and you are happy they are protecting themselves.
- ❑ b) Wait at the front door when your teen gets home from school with the condoms in your hand, and say, "How do you explain this?"
- ❑ c) Wait for a quiet time and talk to your teen about your values about sexual intercourse and protection.

Your son or daughter tells you that he or she is sexually involved and asks you to help them purchase condoms. You:
- ❑ a) Say "Absolutely not. Sex is wrong for someone your age."
- ❑ b) Say, "If you are old enough to have sex, you're old enough to get your own condoms."
- ❑ c) Go with your teen to a drug store that very night.
- ❑ d) Talk to them about their decision making regarding sex and protection, and share your values.

Your daughter (or your son's girlfriend) comes to you and tells you she thinks she is pregnant. You:
- ❑ a) Tell her you will arrange for the abortion.
- ❑ b) Tell her that she must have the baby.
- ❑ c) Ask her what she is thinking about doing.
- ❑ d) Tell her you expect them to get married.

Chapter 5
Late High School
Eleventh and Twelfth Grades

Staying Connected

I want to go back to the first rule of this book. It is critical that you stay involved in your teen's life. Now that your teenager is in the eleventh or twelfth grade, it is going to get harder. In most states, teens begin driving between the ages of 16 and 17. The automobile is your teen's passage to freedom—and time away from you. You may have just lost that precious time alone in the car to talk about important issues.

It is tempting to think that now that your teen is in the eleventh or twelfth grade that you are *done* with the hardest part of parenting. You aren't done. They still need your attention, your time, and your involvement.

Teens want you to ask them about their lives. One 17-year-old girl told me, "Parents should know what their teens are doing so we don't have to lie to you." They want you to trust them, and they want your approval. Some adolescent psychologists suggest that it is much more powerful to tell your teen who has gotten into trouble that you are disappointed in their behavior than it is to ground them.

You will need to make a special effort to stay involved in your teen's life. Try to set aside a time each day, if only for ten minutes, when you can talk to each other about their day. Daily family dinners may be tough given your eleventh or twelfth grader's work and after school schedule, but try for at least a few dinners together as a family each week. Some families have a ritual of Sunday dinners that no one in the family is allowed to miss. Young people who take fewer risks have parents who are there when they wake up, there when they come home from school, there at dinner, and there at bedtime on a regular basis. I know all of these may not be possible; try for as many as you can. The research shows that teenagers who *feel* connected to their parents are actually as secure as those who spend a lot of time together.

Try to find activities for you and your older teen to do together. Maybe it is as simple as asking your teen to go grocery shopping with you each week. Maybe you can take up a hobby together. Maybe it is going to church or synagogue, or sharing a volunteer task together at the community center. Maybe you can go jogging, work out, or play tennis together. Maybe it is a weekly cup of coffee at Starbucks. Think about what works for both of you and what is available in your community.

Support your teen in his or her activities. It is just as important as when they were little to go to their games, their plays, and their recitals. It is still important to go to "back to school" night, although many parents stop going in the last part of high school. It is very important to talk frequently to your teen about their plans for after high school and about how you can support them.

Remember to keep telling your teen that you love them. They still need hugs, and they still need to be reminded about your love, even if it does not seem that way. Their first romantic relationships and their friendships are not replacing their need for you. If anything, they may need your love and guidance more than ever.

First Love

Most teenagers fall in love—head over heels, can't breathe, obsessed love—for the first time in their junior or senior year. Yes, many of them have "gone with" someone before, but it is during the later high school years that they often have their first "in love" experience. Too many parents label this "puppy love." They negate their teen's intense emotional relationship and close off most communication about it.

I want you to think back to your own adolescence for a minute. Who was your first love? Stop reading for a minute and go back and remember him or her. What did your first love look like? Smell like? (I sometimes still get a picture of my first love when I smell "Canoe" on someone!) Where did you meet? Did you wear a ring, ID bracelet, sweater, or something else to "formalize" your relationship? Can you remember what it was like to be in love that first time? Do you remember thinking that no one anywhere had ever had such wonderful, intoxicating feelings? Think about your sexual experiences with that person...what was it like to hold hands? Kiss? Neck for hours? Begin slow exploration of their body? How far did you go sexually in that relationship? What helped you decide how far to go sexually?

Now, try to remember how your own parents reacted to that love relationship. Were they supportive, inviting your first love into your family and home? Were they critical of your choice of partner? Did they try to limit or control your seeing that person? (Did that work? Probably not.) Were they bemused, subtly letting you know that they thought it was cute that you were in love?

Your teenager in love is probably feeling many of the same things you did. First love during the teenage years is often intoxicating...and narcissistic. Because in this period of adolescence, teens are often so self-centered and self-involved, the person they are in love with may serve more as a mirror, reflecting characteristics that your teenager admires rather than seeing the individual who is loved for himself or herself. This love can even seem borderline obsessive: I remember once writing my first love's name in tiny script more than one thousand times on a napkin one afternoon.

Teenagers sometimes lose themselves in their first love. Students begin neglecting their homework; athletes begin not working out as hard; other friends are dropped and ignored. Teens often complain that their friends who are in love no longer have time for them. Time not spent in person with the beloved is often spent on the phone with them, e-mailing them, or daydreaming about them. Unlike couples just a few years younger, these couples do go on dates, and they spend a lot of their free time together. Most, but not all, of these relationships are exclusive and monogamous.

What is a parent to do? First, acknowledge your teen's feelings. Let them know that you were once a teenager too, and that you have had these types of feelings. Try to encourage your teen to talk about their feelings and their relationship. You can ask questions like:

- "Tell me what makes him/her special."
- "What do you most enjoy about him/her?"
- "When you are together, what do you most enjoy doing?"

You may want to share this information from my colleague and friend Sol Gordon about the difference between mature and immature love. Sol says that Immature Love is when the other person's caring for you is a lot more important than your caring for the other person. Your love is a burden on the other person, and the state of being in love is exhausting. Mature Love, he says, is "when your caring about the other person is just a little more important to you than having the other person care for you. The relationship is mutually enhancing and energizing." In other words, when you are in a mature love relationship, you feel great, energized, and alive. When you are in an immature relationship, you feel obsessed, depressed, and cranky. Teenagers—and adults—experience both kinds. You can help your teen evaluate what type of relationship they are in.

Encourage your teen to invite their boyfriend/girlfriend into your home and family life. Get to know your child's partner. Have them over for dinner; invite them to family celebrations; have your teen ask them over to study (when you are home!); include them in family outings. By involving your teen's dating partner in your family life, you are validating your teen's feelings; assessing whether this person genuinely cares about and treats your teen with respect; identifying potential problems; and perhaps reducing the likelihood that your teen will engage in sexual behaviors. You are also staying actively involved in your teen's life. (Go back and reread the opening section of this chapter.)

One caveat here: You want to welcome your child's romantic partner into your home, but you do not want to become overly involved in this relationship. Most teen love relationships last only a few months. One friend of mine reports being brokenhearted when her daughter's boyfriend broke up with her. "I felt badly for Brenda, of course," she reported. "But I felt badly for me too. I really liked Daniel." Do not invest too much until the relationship has gone on for perhaps more than six months. Being open and welcoming is different than developing an independent relationship that you want to last.

Of course, this works best if you like your teen's choice of love interest. What if you don't? One parent told me, "I was happy my child was finally in love, but frankly I just didn't see what she saw in him." Another said, "I'm going crazy. I can't stand my son's girlfriend, yet I want to be supportive of him. Should I let him know how I feel?" Forbidding your teenage child to see someone you don't think is good for them is unlikely to work. (Remember Romeo and Juliet?) In fact, it is likely to mean that they will sneak around behind your back to see their beloved and you will be cut out of this part of your teen's life. Instead, talk to your child about your reactions and listen to them talk about their feelings. Perhaps they see good qualities that you do not readily observe. Perhaps they just want to have a boyfriend or a girlfriend around. Perhaps they are attracted to this person precisely because he or she is so different than what you might hope for!

Although it may be difficult, it can be especially important to include a partner you do not like into your family life. One friend of mine really didn't like his daughter's boyfriend, but they decided to take him away for a weekend getaway anyway. When I asked him why, he said, "I am much more comfortable with the enemy I know, than the enemy I don't know." By treating this person with respect—and having them see how much you value and cherish your child—you are giving them the message that they had better treat your child well.

Conversely, you may not like the way your child is treating a boyfriend or girlfriend. One friend of mine reported to me that it was pretty clear her daughter was just using a new boy to make her last boyfriend jealous. Another's son just thought it was time to have a girlfriend. It could be important to share with your child your observations about their behavior. You could say something like, "It seems like you are pretty sarcastic with your boyfriend/girlfriend. It bothered me to see you acting that way." (Or name whatever behavior it is you did not like observing.) Then, share your ideas and values about the characteristics of a healthy relationship.

Take action if you think your teen is being abused in any way. Dating violence is real. Almost half of girls *and* boys report that they have been hit, slapped, punched, or sexually coerced by their dating partner. It's not only girls that can be victims of dating violence. One parent of a 17-year-old boy told me that he had watched his son's girlfriend hit him. When angry, she would kick, pull his hair, or slap him repeatedly. (If you are observing this type of behavior, you may want to skip ahead to the Special Issues section on date rape and violence on pages 189 to 193.)

Encourage your teen to stay involved with other activities and with other friends. It is never a good idea at any age to give up everything for any single relationship. It is wonderful to be in love at any age, but it is almost always a mistake to be in a relationship with one person that precludes everyone else in your life, no matter how terrific it is. Make sure your in-love children continue to see their friends, continue to study, continue to attend church or temple youth group, continue their hobbies, and stay involved in family life.

The reality is that most teen love relationships will come to an end. Being sure that your teen is not giving up the rest of his life while he is in love will make surviving the inevitable breakup easier.

Just as it is important to take your child's love seriously, it is equally critical to take their broken heart seriously. Last year, I was on *Oprah* with a group of teenagers who had tried to commit suicide after the end of a romantic relationship. The data are actually pretty frightening: 33 to 40 percent of teen suicides have to do with a failed romantic relationship.

Think back for a minute to your first broken heart. (I'm assuming here you have had your heart broken. On the *Oprah* show, only one woman in the audience raised her hand when we asked, "Is there anyone here who hasn't had her heart broken?") I remember weeping uncontrollably when my 16-year-old love broke up with me. (Interestingly, we have different memories about why we broke up. We have recently reconnected through the Internet and I had dinner with him and his wife while I was in their city on a business trip. I remember we broke up because I wouldn't go further sexually; he remembers just getting a crush on another young woman and thinking it was time to try someone new.)

Right after a breakup, your child is likely to be depressed, withdrawn, and unlikely to sleep or eat well. This is a normal reaction to grieving the end of a relationship. Offer them extra TLC (tender, loving care). Sometimes, it helps to just hold them. Or sit and listen to them. Plan a special outing that you know they will like or indulge them with small gifts or special meals. Let them know you have survived a broken heart yourself. Encourage them to be with other friends (this is where not giving up your friends when you *are* in love really helps). It definitely does not help to say things like, "There are other fish in the sea," or "He/she really wasn't worth you anyway." Acknowledge and support how difficult the end of a relationship can be.

Most teenagers will begin to return to their normal selves within a few weeks of the breakup. But for some teenagers, the end of the relationship can be the beginning of a clinical depression. If your child is not getting out of the house or beginning to put the relationship behind them in a few weeks, they may have become clinically (not just situationally) depressed. Signs of clinical depression include diminished interest in activities, significant weight loss, insomnia, loss of energy, feelings of worthlessness and guilt, agitation, constant headaches or stomachaches, pessimism that their life will never get better, and recurrent thoughts of suicide or death.

If this seems to describe your child after a breakup (or indeed at any time for more than a couple of weeks), they and you need outside help. Contact the school guidance department or social worker or your local health department or mental health agency for a referral to a psychiatrist, psychologist, or social worker who specializes in working with teenagers.

Breakups may be even harder if your teen has had a serious sexual relationship with a partner.

Sexual Behavior: What to Expect

You're probably not going to like reading this, but the fact is that your 16- or 17-year-old in-love teenager is likely to be having—or about to have—sexual intercourse for the first time. The average age of first sexual intercourse in the United States is about 16 for boys and 17 for girls. In studies asking teens why they have sex, the majority of teens who have intercourse say they do it to express their love for their partner. The majority of teens say they do not feel peer or partner pressure to have intercourse. Typically, girls are more likely to say that they are having intercourse because they are in love than boys are: 71 percent of girls said they were in love with their last sexual partner compared to 45 percent of boys.

My experience with teens in the last years of high school—and validated by many of the focus group studies that I have read—is that they make a distinction between sexual intercourse and other sexual behaviors, including oral sex. Sexual intercourse is reserved for serious relationships; one teen girl told me that it was just too much of a risk and too much trouble in high school. But, she anticipated engaging in other sexual behaviors, including probably oral sex. This may be hard for adults with teens to read, but "hooking up" or "getting play"—which according to one teen boy ranges from "making out to serious oral sex"—in many teens' worlds is considered fun, common, and can take place with someone they never expect to see again. Both boys and girls can hook up as long as they do not do it too often. Girls need to avoid being labeled as "sluts"; boys need to avoid being labeled as "players"; sexual adventurers with lots of partners or those who have intercourse outside of relationships are "dirty kids." Yes, it is a different world than when we were teens; perhaps we could kiss someone we weren't serious about, but oral sex was definitely a bigger deal than it is today.

Many eleventh- and twelfth-grade virgins are surprisingly sexually sophisticated. Although many virgins have little sexual experience, by senior year, one-third of the teens who had not had penile-vaginal intercourse had masturbated a partner and/or had been masturbated by a partner. Ten percent had experienced fellatio with ejaculation, and 13 percent had experienced cunnilingus. White teen virgins are more sexually experienced that African-American and Hispanic teen virgins.

Penile-vaginal intercourse is often reserved for a love relationship, and these very sophisticated teens also report a very sweet yearning for love without sex. One eleventh-grade boy told me, "Holding hands and watching a movie with the girl you love is the coolest thing in the world...and so much better than a blow job from a hook up."

The major exception to sexual intercourse in serious relationships for many young people is first intercourse at the junior or senior prom. Along with the limos, dinners, and flowers, alcohol and sex are often an assumed part of prom night. This is not a new phenomenon. When I worked at Planned Parenthood two decades ago, we saw more girls for pregnancy tests in late June (six weeks after the proms) than at any other time. Many communities give out cards with the numbers of taxis along with tuxedo rentals to cut down on the number of teens drinking on prom night and driving. I've often thought they should be giving out condoms as well.

Pressure to go to the prom with someone special is intense, partly as result of the "sex on prom night" assumption. One tenth-grade friend of mine had just started seeing a junior right before prom night. She asked her new boyfriend whether they would be "doing what everyone else was" after the prom was over. She was talking about the after-prom parties; he thought she was talking about sex, and said, "Gee, Hilary, I'm not sure we're ready." A group of junior girls in my town last year decided to avoid this pressure, but they still wanted to go to the prom. They decided they would go together in a group rather than on dates with young men. They went shopping together and bought new dresses, rented the limo for the six of them, took themselves out to dinner, and had a great time. Proms can be especially difficult for gay and lesbian teens, who may feel pressure to conform to heterosexual dates or who have to be really brave in most places to go with a date of the same sex.

The important thing to do is to talk to your teen in the spring around prom time. Many communities have abandoned proms, but they are still widely popular. Talk to your teen about your expectations about alcohol, driving, and sex on prom night. Be explicit about where they can go after the prom and how late they can come home. (In many communities *not* coming home is part of the prom ritual, but do you really want your 16-year-old in a hotel room with her boyfriend?) If your teen is not going to the prom, be sure to talk to them about their feelings as well. I know these may be difficult talks, but prom definitely presents a teachable moment.

Here is what the research tells us about teens and heterosexual behavior. (I deal with homosexual behavior and teens in the section "Dad, I Think I'm Gay" on page 181.) By senior year in high school, six in ten high school students report that they have had sexual intercourse, with roughly the same percentages of boys and girls having had this experience. Between the junior and senior years of high school, there is a sharp jump in the percentage of teens who are sexually experienced: In eleventh grade, only half of teens report that they have had intercourse, but by the end of senior year, nearly two-thirds have done so. More than one in five seniors report that they have had four or more partners in their lifetime. Still, remember that one-third of high school seniors have not had intercourse.

How did you feel reading these statistics? Did you think to yourself, "not my daughter" or "not my son" or did you think, "That's about what I would expect?" My observation is that parents, in general, adopt one of three positions when it comes to their teens and sexual relationships.

Many parents want their teenager to abstain from sexual behaviors: In one national survey, 95 percent of adults said that teenage sexual relationships are always wrong. But parents vary tremendously about what constitutes abstinence: Is it okay if their teens kiss and make out? Touch each other's genitals? Masturbate each other to orgasm? Have oral sex? Do everything *but* have intercourse? And until when: Senior prom? College? Age 21? Their wedding night? Take the time to think about what abstinence for your high school student means to you.

Other parents adopt what I call the "don't ask, don't tell" posture. They have a pretty good idea that their teenager is engaging in some types of sexual behaviors; they just do not want to know about it. And they certainly don't want the behavior to happen in their home. As one mom of a 16-year-old boy told me, "I'm pretty sure that they are having sex. I know they are using condoms. But, I don't want it to be happening in his bedroom while I'm downstairs cooking dinner!" Another parent, who is single and dates, said to me, "It's like we have a deal. I don't ask her about her sex life and she doesn't ask me about mine."

Some parents seem to be happily content with being unaware of their children's sexual behavior. Let me give you an example. A few weeks ago, I was giving a series of workshops at an upscale health resort. The room was full of adults, largely between the ages of 30 and 60, and I was leading a pretty explicit adult sexual enrichment workshop. At the end, two women came up to me to tell me that they had brought their 17-year-old daughters to the workshop and that they were happy to have had them there. (The daughters apparently were sitting on the floor so I had not noticed the teens in the crowded room.) I told the moms that I hoped that they were all right with the frankness of this workshop, as it was very different than one I would do for high school seniors.

After almost everyone else had left the room, two very

attractive teens made their way towards me. They asked shyly, "Can we ask you something?" "Sure," I smiled. "Can you tell us about how to make oral sex more pleasurable for the boy?" the red-haired one asked. I then talked with them a bit, reminding them that I had said earlier that oral sex poses risks of sexually transmitted diseases (something neither of them knew) and that they should not get semen in their mouths. "But," the brunette answered, "What do you do if your boyfriend tells you that you have to?" It was clear to me that this was a situation she had faced. "But what if he doesn't come? He's told me that he gets 'blue balls.'" And the discussion continued, with me assuring her that erections did go away by themselves, and that he could always go home and masturbate after their date if he was uncomfortable.

The next day, I saw the mother of one of the girls. She again thanked me for the workshop and how glad she was that she had brought her daughter. She then said to me, "She's so innocent. I don't think she's even kissed yet." I thought to myself, "Oh, yes, she has…" but simply encouraged her to use this opportunity to have some frank discussions with her daughter.

There are still other parents who are much more open and accepting of their teens' sexual involvement and experimentation. One mom told me, "I started having sex at 15, and I enjoyed it. How can I tell my son and my daughter that this isn't a good idea?" Another told me that she wanted her teenage sons' initial sexual experiences to be positive: "That meant that I was willing to accept what was right for them." She remembers one of her sons, when he was a junior, saying to her, "You know, mom, we are being careful…and I'm really happy." She responded, "Thank you for sharing with that with me…I'm glad for you."

The point is that you need to think about where you are on this continuum, and talk with your teen. If your teen is in a serious romantic relationship, I'm going to suggest that you sit down and have a heart-to-heart talk with your child about sex. This may be one of the only times I will suggest to you that you have a specific one-to-one, deliberate talk about sex. Yes, a talk about sex—not sexuality—but specific sexual behaviors, decisions, pleasure, and protection. And I'm not sure I know how to make this easy for either of you. Your request to have this talk is likely to be met with "Oh, mom/dad, do we have to? We've already talked about all this."

But, this is a key moment to reinforce your feelings about teenage sexual intercourse and abstinence, and to make sure that if your teen is having intercourse or planning to do so soon, that they are using contraception and condoms. It is a good time to talk about the characteristics of a sexually healthy relationship and how your child is making sexual decisions. You can also use it as an opportunity to talk about pleasure with your child and the importance of respecting his or her partner.

Perhaps you can use this book as an opening: "I read in a book that many teenagers who are in love the way you and Chris are begin to have sexual intercourse. I want to remind you that I/we think that teenagers your age are too young for the responsibilities that come with sexual intercourse." (Or "...that we hope you will be married before you have intercourse," or whatever your values are about premarital sex.) Let me remind you again about the good news about reinforcing an abstinence message even with in-love teenagers: Teens who say they have received a clear message about abstaining from intercourse from their parents are more likely to abstain than teens who have not had that discussion with their parents.

But I'm going to suggest to you that in today's world, it is absolutely critical that your child knows that if they do have intercourse, whether you approve or not of their decision, that they know you want them to use contraception and condoms. As I will discuss in greater depth below, unplanned pregnancies and sexually transmitted diseases are rampant among sexually active young people. Four in ten teenage girls who have sexual intercourse during their teen years will become pregnant, and one in four sexually active teen men and teen women will get a sexually transmitted disease.

Talking About Contraception and STD Prevention

Fortunately, the good news is that there has been a dramatic increase in the number of young people using contraception in the past decade. More than three-quarters of teens now use a contraceptive method at first intercourse, compared to less than half who used a method a decade ago. Most used a method at last intercourse. In fact, teens today are much more likely to use a contraceptive method than we were three decades ago.

The majority of juniors and seniors who are sexually involved are protecting themselves with condoms: Nearly 70 percent used a condom at first intercourse. But still, the problem is that one-third of teens who are having sex use contraceptives inconsistently, and some do not use anything at all. And let me remind you: Nine in ten women who have sex for a year without contraception will get pregnant.

This is where you may have a role to play. Many teenagers don't use a contraceptive method because they are afraid their parents will find out. In my talks for the past fifteen years, I have asked teens, parents, and health and education professionals all over the country to finish this sentence: "A teenage girl with a condom in her purse is a _____." The answer (indeed the thought you probably just had) is a "*slut.*" Not a smart girl, not a girl who is prepared, not a girl who is taking care of herself, but a *slut*. It is a wonder that so many teens actually do carry and use condoms despite this sense of cultural disapproval.

It *is* possible to tell your child that you hope that they won't have intercourse and that if they do you want them to protect themselves against pregnancy and disease. You can say something like: "We really don't believe that teens your age should engage in sexual intercourse. We know that you are in love and you are probably experimenting with sexual behaviors. We hope that you will choose behaviors that don't pose any risks to you or your partner. We hope that if you decide to have intercourse, you will make sure that you always use birth control and condoms. I'm wondering if you've thought about contraception and how you might get condoms and birth control."

Notice that I said "condoms *and* birth control." Unlike when many of us were young adults, it is critical today that young people who are having intercourse protect themselves against both pregnancy and sexually transmitted diseases. Condoms are the only currently available protection we have against most sexually transmitted diseases. Condoms are not 100 percent effective at preventing STDs, but if intercourse is going to occur, using one is *ten thousand times* safer than not using one at all. That bears repeating: Using a condom is ten thousand times safer than not using one. Condoms significantly reduce the risk of HIV transmission: In one study of heterosexual couples where one partner was HIV positive and one was HIV negative, none of the HIV negative people were infected who used condoms consistently for vaginal and anal intercourse.

It is true that condoms do not protect against diseases such as lice, scabies, herpes, and warts (HPV) that are not covered by the condom (such as those that are found on the thigh, scrotum, vulva). It is important that your teen also learn to *look* at a partner's genital area before having intercourse, condom or no condom. And that they have at least an annual physical that includes screening for sexually transmitted diseases.

Condoms are less effective at protecting against pregnancies than sexually transmitted diseases. Under ideal conditions in a laboratory, condoms are 98 percent effective in blocking the passage of sperm. But reality rarely mimics such laboratory conditions. In actual use, condoms are about 88 percent effective in preventing pregnancies during the first year of use. Failure rates through breakage and slippage are much higher in newer users.

Here are the basic directions for condom use that I have adapted from the authors of *Contraceptive Technology* that a sexually active teenager (indeed an adult!) needs to know:

- Use a new condom with every act of sexual intercourse, from start to finish.
- Only use latex or polyurethane condoms. Animal skin condoms do *not* provide any protection against sexually transmitted diseases.
- Store condoms in a cool place out of direct sunlight, and not in a wallet or glove compartment. Do not use damaged, discolored, brittle, or sticky condoms.
- Check the expiration date on the package to make sure it has not passed.

- Carefully open the condom package; teeth and finger-nails can tear a condom. If a condom rips or tears, take out another one or postpone intercourse. It's a good idea to have several condoms on hand.
- Put on the condom after the penis is erect and before it touches any part of the partner's body. If a penis is uncircumcised, pull back the foreskin before putting on the condom.
- Unroll the condom a little bit to make sure the condom is being unrolled in the right direction. The rolled ring should be on the outside. Be sure you are putting on the condom the right way. If the condom doesn't unroll easily on the penis, it is probably on upside-down. Throw it away and begin again.
- If you need additional lubrication, use a condom lubricated with a spermicidal or a water-based lubricant like Astroglide. Other lubricants, such as Vaseline, cooking oil, baby oil, or hand lotions, will weaken the condom.
- Put on the condom by pinching the reservoir tip and unrolling it all the way down the shaft of the penis from the head to the base. If a condom does not have a reservoir tip, leave a half-inch space at the head of the penis for the semen to collect after ejaculation.
- Very soon after ejaculation, and before the penis becomes flaccid, withdraw the penis while it is still erect, holding on to the condom at the base to prevent slippage and leakage.
- Wrap the used condom in tissue and discard it in a wastebasket. Do not flush condoms in the toilet or leave them on the ground.

(For more information on the other contraceptive methods,

check out the Planned Parenthood website, www.plannedparenthood.org.)

Many parents have asked me, "Should I buy condoms for my sexually active teenagers?" Some parents would be appalled at this thought. Others are so concerned about sexually transmitted diseases that they put aside their discomfort. One teen boy told me that his parents bought him a gross of condoms as a Christmas present, with a note that said, "Just in case." He thought it was pretty cool. One mom I know solved the condom problem by buying a large box of condoms and putting them in the linen closet. She told her sons that it was there, for them or for them to give their friends, and there would be no questions asked about where or how they were used.

A friend of mine called me last May and asked if we could get together to talk. Her son, Roberto, was planning to go away from home at the end of June to be a counselor at a remote summer camp. Up until now, he had not had a girlfriend and had not expressed much interest in dating. But he was 16, and she and her husband were disagreeing about whether they should send him to camp with a talk and a packet of condoms. I've had similar discussions with parents of juniors and seniors who are sending their teens on teen-only adventure trips, band trips, or weeks in Europe.

What's going on here? Parents who might not think of supplying their teens with condoms for the junior prom are worried that their teen will fall in love and become sexually involved for the first time when they are away from home in a semi-independent status. And their concern is probably not ill founded: After all, sometime between junior year and graduation, many young people will experience their first romantic relationship that includes sexual intercourse.

But as my friend said to me, "I don't want him to think that we are expecting him to have sex." Other parents wonder whether talking to their sons or daughters about condoms or indeed actually supplying them might actually encourage their child to experiment with intercourse.

I first encouraged my friend to talk with her husband about their family values about teen intercourse. Were they comfortable with the idea that their son might begin having intercourse? Did they think their son was emotionally mature enough to handle a relationship that included intercourse? Would their son have an easy way to obtain condoms if he did decide to become sexually involved?

I encouraged her to plan a quiet time where the three of them could discuss his upcoming summer. It was important for them to share their values about premarital sexual involvement. It was important for them to talk with their son about the characteristics of a sexually mature relationship.

And, if they thought their son might become sexually involved this summer, it was probably a good idea to talk to him about condoms. One study found that when parents talk to their teens about condom use *before* they have their first sexual intercourse, the teens are much more likely to use a condom at *first* intercourse. In fact, teens whose parents have talked to them about intercourse are far more likely than other teens to use condoms throughout their teen years.

It *is* possible to tell your child that you hope that they won't have intercourse, and that if they do you want them to protect themselves against pregnancy and disease. You can say something like: "We really don't believe that teens your age should engage in sexual intercourse. We know that while you are away, you may become involved with someone romantically and want to experiment with sexual behaviors. We hope that you will choose behaviors that don't pose any risks to you or your partner. We hope that if you decide to have intercourse, you will make sure that you and your partner are both ready for a mature sexual relationship. That means making sure that you are at least using condoms for disease and pregnancy prevention. We're wondering if you would like to bring some condoms with you to camp just in case this happens."

They might also want to ask their son if he would like their help in purchasing condoms before he leaves for camp. In general, I think that teens who are mature enough to have sexual intercourse are mature enough to purchase their own condoms. But it is also true that the first visit to a drug store to buy condoms can be pretty unnerving, and it might be supportive to ask them if they want help.

One adult male friend of mine told me that when he unpacked at camp the summer of his senior year of high school several packages of condoms fell out on the floor. One of his parents apparently slipped them into his duffel bag when he was finished packing. He was mortified when the other counselor saw them! He also remembers feeling that he was letting his father down all summer. I certainly don't recommend supplying your son or daughter with contraceptives without their permission or their involvement!

Other Methods of Birth Control

Because condoms are less effective at preventing pregnancies, teenage women who are having heterosexual intercourse must also use a more effective birth control method to assure that they do not become pregnant. The most effective methods for teenagers are hormonal contraceptives (the birth control pill, patch, and NuvaRing), Depo Provera (a shot that is given every three months that is 99.7 percent effective), and implants.

Among sexually active 15 to 19 year olds, here is what contraceptive method they used at last intercourse:

- 23 percent birth control pills
- 28 percent condoms
- 8 percent Depo Provera or implants
- 4 percent withdrawal
- 6 percent other methods.

All of these methods—except withdrawal and condoms—require a prescription or a trip to the doctor or family planning clinic. If your daughter or son is having sex, you need to think about how much help you want to give them in obtaining contraception or condoms. Some parents believe that if their child is old enough to be having intercourse, they are certainly old enough to obtain and pay for their own contraceptive methods. Other parents want to know for sure that their child is using a method and may want to help them pick out the best method for them. You need to think about how you want to handle this, and talk to your teen about how they will decide about contraception and how they will arrange to get it.

Parents also need to talk with their teenage sons and daughters about withdrawal and about emergency contraception. About 4 percent of sexually involved teens use withdrawal. Now, you may have heard the joke, "What do you call people who practice withdrawal?" The answer is "parents." But withdrawal is actually a pretty effective method of contraception. If used perfectly, withdrawal is about 96 percent effective at preventing pregnancy. The advantage to teens is that it is free, always available, and relatively easy to use. I want all sexually active teens to know that in the words of one HIV prevention poster, "no glove, no love." But, I also want them to know that if they are going to have intercourse anyway, condom or no condom, they must at least practice withdrawal. The major disadvantage for teens is that in order for withdrawal to be effective, the man must recognize that he is about to ejaculate and withdraw completely from the vagina and ejaculate away from the vulva. Many teen boys just do not have this type of control. And, of course, withdrawal provides no protection against STDs.

Teenagers also need to know about emergency contraception. The reality is that condoms break; teenagers forget their pills; the man ejaculates too close to the vulva; a couple who has pledged abstinence has intercourse anyway. Emergency contraception involves taking two birth control pills within seventy-two hours of unprotected intercourse. It is only 74 percent effective at preventing pregnancy, so it should never be relied on as a primary method of contraception, and of course, it provides no protection against sexually transmitted diseases. But, if a pregnancy is likely, it is certainly worth trying. There is a toll-free number (1-888-NOT2-LATE) to find doctors, pharmacies, and clinics near you who prescribe emergency contraception.

I know talking about contraception and condoms can be difficult for even the most progressive parent. It means acknowledging that your son or daughter is sexually involved in a pretty intimate relationship. It may mean putting aside your hopes that they would wait until they were married to first have intercourse—or at least wait until they got out of high school. But talking about these issues with them also tells them that you care about their health and their future, and helps assure you that they won't be faced with an unplanned pregnancy, or sexually transmitted disease.

Finding Condoms or Pills in Your Teen's Room

Some parents never do talk to their teens about contraception. One day, they just discover condoms or birth control pills in their teen's bedroom, purse, or pant's pockets. Of course, one has to ask why the parent was in their teen's bedroom drawers, purse, or wallet...but nevertheless, it happens. And some teens in my experience seem to leave their birth control pills or condoms around precisely so that mom and dad can find them.

Okay, mom and dad, the first thing to do if this happens to you is take a deep breath. Try to remain calm. Remind yourself for just for a minute that your son or daughter is acting responsibly by using protection against pregnancy or STDs.

The reality is that most parents are going to be pretty shaken by this. One mom told me, "I had no idea that she was having sex...and I just wasn't ready for evidence of it." A dad said, "I hate that he didn't come to me first to talk about it." One parent told me, "My first thought was I wanted to kill her...and her boyfriend."

Directly confronting your child with what you found is unlikely to have positive results. You could be told, "I'm holding on to them for a friend." Or, "Nothing's happening; I'm taking them to clear up my skin," or "Mom, they gave them to me in health class; I'm not using them."

I once heard Robert Haas, the former president of Levi Strauss, the company that makes blue jeans, tell one of the funniest stories I've heard about this situation. He received an angry letter from a father. It said something like, "Yesterday, when I was doing the laundry, I found a condom in my son's 504 jeans. When I asked him about it, he told me that the company is now including a condom in the pocket of every new pair of Levis. I demand that you stop this immoral practice now!"

Well, of course, Levi Strauss wasn't packaging condoms into their new pants for sale. (Although the company has been one of the most involved corporations in the fight against AIDS.) Haas said that what he wanted to do was write the man back a letter and point out the obvious: The man's son was having sex, and he should be rewarding him for being responsible. At minimum, he should be talking to him! Instead, as I recall, he had customer service write him back and tell the father that this was indeed not a company promotion.

So, what do you do? Well, some parents will feel comfortable using the direct approach. You certainly have been presented with a teachable moment: "Honey, I was putting away your laundry today, and came across pills/condoms. I think it's time we talked." And then you both share your feelings and values about your child engaging in these types of mature sexual behaviors as well as supporting them for taking responsibility for themselves.

That last may be hard for some parents. You are against premarital sex; you hate even the thought that your child is doing more than kissing. Maybe your child isn't even in a relationship and you are aghast that they could be one of the teens who have casual sexual encounters.

I understand all of those feelings. But remember, this is their health and future you are dealing with. If your teen is having intercourse of any kind, even if you positively hate the thought, isn't it better that they are protecting themselves against pregnancy and/or disease? What happens when they don't protect themselves? Nine in ten sexually active teenage women who do not use a contraceptive method will be pregnant in a year.

"Mom, I Think I'm Pregnant"

Your teenager comes to you, pale and shaking. "Mom, Dad, I don't know how to tell you this. I think I'm pregnant." Or "Mom, Dad, I think my girlfriend is pregnant." Six percent of all high school students say that they have been pregnant or gotten someone pregnant.

Each year, just under nine hundred thousand teenage girls will become pregnant. Put another way, each year one out of every eight teen women in the United States becomes pregnant. Almost all of these teenage pregnancies are unplanned. A little more than half will end in a birth; one-third will end in abortions; one in six will end with a miscarriage.

Despite what you may have read in the news, teenage pregnancy rates and teenage birth rates are declining. Birth rates for all teenagers ages 15 to 19 declined every year from 1991 to 2003. The latest data indicates that teenage birth rates are at their lowest in sixty-five years. In fact, it may surprise you to know that the highest teen birth rate in the United States was in 1957, when many of us were born! The difference is that our teen moms were probably married; only 15 percent of teen births in 1960 were out-of-wedlock, compared to more than three-quarters today. Teenage pregnancy rates are down from a peak of 62 per 1,000 in 1991 to a low of 40 per 1,000 teen girls today.

But, none of that matters if it is your teenager sitting there who has just said, "I think I'm pregnant." There isn't any way I can prepare you for that moment. A minute ago, you probably didn't even know that your child was sexually involved. Now, you know they are, and they are involved in a pregnancy. You may feel shock, disappointment, and grief. You want to scream, "How could this possibly have happened?" Your mind races, seeing your child's future eclipsed. You worry about what the neighbors will think, what your church will think, what *your* mother will think. You will want to take the time to think through and sort out *your* feelings, but for now, you need to concentrate on your child.

Take a deep breath. Try to be calm. You first need to listen. You might try saying something like, "Tell me why you think you might be pregnant." "Tell me what happened." "Tell me what you are feeling right now." "Tell me what you think you want to do."

Your daughter (or your son's girlfriend) may have missed a period and may not know for sure that she is pregnant. Offer to help her confirm her pregnancy. Over the counter home pregnancy tests are available at almost all drug stores, and they are about 85 percent accurate in detecting a positive pregnancy. The most common problem with a home pregnancy test is a negative result because the test was performed too early in the pregnancy. Clinics and physicians offer an inexpensive pregnancy test that can provide accurate results as early as one week after fertilization, or one week before the missed period. If the home pregnancy test is negative, and your daughter is having early signs of pregnancy, like breast tenderness, nausea, and urinary frequency, have her get a test at a clinic anyway.

Your daughter has basically three options in dealing with an unintended pregnancy. She can continue the pregnancy and raise the child (either alone or with her partner), she can continue the pregnancy and give the baby up for adoption, or she can have an abortion.

Note that I said *your daughter* has three options. As much as you may want to be involved, as much as you may want to make this decision, it is hers alone to make ultimately. You may have the right in your state to give your consent for her abortion, but you do not have to give her permission for her to carry the pregnancy to term or to give the baby up for adoption.

If it is your son who has impregnated his girlfriend, he may want to be involved in the decision, he may have strong feelings about how he wants this decision to be made, but it is ultimately the young woman's choice alone to make. Her decision will affect your life and his life. (If she chooses to have the baby, he will have some financial accountability in every state in America.) Interestingly, boys and parents' positions are reversed. He has no legal right to stop her from having an abortion, but he can stop her from giving the baby up for adoption.

However, that isn't to say as the parent that you don't have an important role to play. Your teen needs you right now. He or she will need help figuring out the alternatives and consequences of this decision. If possible, try to involve the boy in these discussions about decisions, no matter how angry you feel towards him right now. Remind yourself that he didn't get her pregnant alone! Ideally, both sets of parents will be involved in these conversations.

No decisions have to be made overnight, but the decision needs to be reached as soon as possible. Abortion is safest in the first twelve weeks of pregnancy. Medical abortion (abortions through a pill not a surgical procedure) needs to be done in the first seven weeks. If there is a chance that your teen will continue the pregnancy, she needs to begin prenatal care as soon as possible and to take care of herself and the pregnancy.

There are resources in your community that can help your daughter with her decision. Most Planned Parenthood clinics and other family planning clinics offer pregnancy counseling. A mental health professional or member of the clergy may be helpful. I would recommend that you avoid places labeled "pregnancy crisis centers" for help in decision making. According to the authors of *Contraceptive Technology*, "These agencies do not provide the nonjudgmental environment that [women]…are entitled to have in making a personal decision about pregnancy."

Here are some general questions that I've adapted from the Planned Parenthood Federation of America for you and your teen to consider:

- Which of these choices—having the baby, adoption, or abortion—can I live with?
- Which of these choices are impossible for me?
- How will each of these choices affect my life? The life of the father? My parent's lives?
- What are my plans and hopes for my future? How will a baby change these plans?
- What does my religion and values tell me about these options?
- What will be best for me in the long run?
- Can I provide a loving, stable home for a baby right now?

A little more than half of all pregnant teenagers will choose to have the baby. The results of a teenage birth are lifelong. Having a baby as a teenager is a risk both to the teenager and her baby. The research is pretty clear that parenting teens have lower family incomes, are more likely to be poor, more likely to receive welfare, and less likely to be married than women who have their first children in their twenties, even when compared to teens from similar economic backgrounds. The children of teenage mothers are more likely to do poorly in school and often become teen parents themselves.

Babies born to women under 18 are more likely to be premature and more likely to be small for their gestational age. The risk to the baby if the mom is 18 or 19 is lower, but still higher than for women in their early twenties. The good news though is that a teenager can have a healthy pregnancy—*if* she receives good prenatal care. The problem is that many teen women do not receive prenatal care early enough in their pregnancies because they haven't recognized they are pregnant or have tried to conceal their pregnancies.

But the data are also very clear: Teenagers can have healthy pregnancies and be good parents if they receive adequate support. Good prenatal and obstetrical care are essential to the health of the mom and her baby. One of the most important ways to assure your daughter's future is for her to stay in school and finish her high school education. Title IX requires schools to provide education for pregnant teenagers. Call your local school board to discuss what is available for your child; they must find a way to help her stay in school. Your teen will also need to think through their options for child care, financial issues, medical care, parenting classes, and emotional support.

Teenagers considering having a baby and raising it— whether as a single parent or as a couple—can ask themselves these types of questions:

- Are we ready to put school and college on hold, or is there a realistic way to continue our education?
- Will family members be supportive and help us take care of the child?
- Is there someone who can take care of the child while I'm at school or work or if I get sick?
- Do we have the money to raise a child?
- Am I willing to put my child's needs ahead of my own?
- Are we willing to give up hanging out with our friends, dates, dances, and other teen activities?
- Are we being pressured to keep the baby?
- Are we emotionally mature enough to take care of a baby?

- Do we understand that a child is a responsibility for the rest of our lives?
- What role will my partner have in raising this child? What can I realistically count on?
- Should we be talking about getting married? Would we get married if I weren't pregnant? Am I prepared to be a single parent if things don't work out between us?
- Do I want to be a parent for the rest of my life?

Unlike thirty years ago, most teenagers do not get married after they find out they are pregnant. Today, the majority of teens who parent do so out-of-wedlock. (I use "out-of-wedlock" on purpose. I hate the term "illegitimate child." In my way of thinking, there are no babies born who are not legitimate and worthy of being treated with dignity and respect.) Forty years ago, only one in six babies born to teens were out-of-wedlock. Today, almost three-quarters of them are. If your teen is thinking about getting married, you should know that most teen marriages that happen because of a pregnancy end in divorce. Most teens just are not ready for the responsibilities of parenthood and marriage. You, of course, will need to discuss your family values about marriage and parenthood with your child. Try to help them assess if their relationship is strong enough and good enough to consider marriage at this time.

Some teenagers in considering having a child will decide that they want to have the baby and put it up for adoption. This is not a very popular choice. Most teenagers do not place their children up for adoption. Although there is no national government data on adoption, it is estimated that less than two percent of pregnant women will give their babies up for adoption.

Here are some questions adapted from Planned Parenthood

Federation of America for your teen to think about in considering adoption as an alternative:

- Can you accept the idea of your child being raised by someone else?
- Are you committed to getting good prenatal care?
- Are you choosing adoption because abortion scares you?
- Is the fetus's father supportive of adoption as a choice?
- Is anyone pressuring you to choose adoption?
- Do you respect women who place their children for adoption?
- Do you think you might change your mind after delivery?
- Do you think you will feel good about knowing that your baby is loved and in a good home?

There are two types of adoption to consider: closed adoption and open adoption. In a closed adoption, the names of the adoptive parents and the birth mother are kept secret from each other. Your teen will never know her or his child or the identity of the adoptive parents. In an open adoption, your teen (with your help, I hope) may actually select the adoptive parents for her baby. They may choose to get to know each other; the adoptive parents may help with the pregnancy and childbirth. They also could choose to have an ongoing relationship.

Adoptions are generally arranged in one of three ways. Most adoptions go through a licensed adoption agency. These agencies are licensed by the government to select parents for the baby, handle the legal matters, and assist the teen with the birth and financial matters. Generally, adoptions handled by adoption agencies are closed adoptions. The National Council for Adoption hotline can refer you and your teen to licensed agencies in your area: (202) 328-8072; the Web address is www.ncfa-usa.org. Independent adoptions are arranged by a doctor or a lawyer who knows a couple who want to adopt. Independent adoptions are not legal in all states; if you go this route, make sure that your daughter is represented by her own lawyer to be sure that she is protected. These adoptions are generally open adoptions, and often the adoptive parents will pay for the pregnant teen's medical and hospital bills. For information and referrals about independent adoptions, call the Independent Adoption Center hotline, 1-800-877-OPEN, website www.adoptionhelp.org. In some cases, other relatives in the family are available to adopt the teen's baby. A state agency and a judge must still approve of these adoptions.

It is important that you and your daughter know that adoption is legally binding and a permanent decision. After the baby is born, and after home studies are done, your daughter will need to sign "relinquishment papers." There is a very small window in which she can change her mind. I was surprised to find out that in most states a minor can relinquish her baby without her parent's consent. On the other hand, the baby's father must be involved; in many states, the baby's father can demand custody unless he has also signed release papers for the adoption. Adoption laws are different in every state. Find out the law in your state. Try to talk with a lawyer or adoption counselor before your daughter signs any papers.

The last option available to your daughter is abortion. In 1996, more than 274,000 teenage women had abortions. As surprisingly high as that might seem, the abortion rate has actually been declining among teens for years. Upper-class and middle-class teenagers are much more likely to choose abortion than lower-income teens. Seventy-five percent of pregnant girls from higher-income families will choose abortion compared to fewer than half from lower-income families.

The major reasons teens give for choosing abortion is that they are concerned about how a baby will change their life; they do not feel that they are mature enough to have a child; and they do not feel that they can financially support a child. Here are some questions that your daughter will want to think about before deciding to have an abortion:

1. Is anyone pressuring me to have an abortion?
2. Do my religious beliefs support my having an abortion?
3. Do I respect women who have had an abortion?
4. Will I be able to handle the abortion experience?
5. What do my partner and my parents think about abortion?
6. Am I certain that I want to end this pregnancy?

You do not need to give your permission for your daughter to get pregnant, have a child, or give a child up for adoption. But in more than half of the states in the U.S. (twenty-nine), you will have to give permission for your child to have an abortion. You may be surprised to know that almost two-thirds of girls who have abortions have at least one parent who knows and is supportive.

If your daughter is considering having an abortion, it is safest if it can be done in the first twelve weeks of pregnancy. Early abortion is usually done through a procedure known as "vacuum aspiration." The surgery is extremely safe, and takes only about five minutes. Less than one percent of early abortion patients experience medical complications; in fact, childbirth is ten times more likely to cause a death than an early abortion. It is generally done in a clinic or doctor's office. Generally, an early abortion costs under $500; support may be available for women who can't afford one.

Medical abortion is now available in the United States. In a medical abortion, a woman takes pills to induce the end of the pregnancy. You may have heard of mifepristone, referred to as RU 486. Your local Planned Parenthood can tell you if medical abortion is available in your area.

Your daughter can get abortion assistance at many Planned Parenthood clinics, family planning clinics, women's health clinics, and local departments of health or social services. For a list of Planned Parenthood clinics that offer abortions, you can call 1-800-230-PLAN. For a list of licensed abortion clinics, call the National Abortion Federation Hotline, at 1-800-772-9100.

In some cases, you may not find out your daughter is pregnant until way past the first trimester. Some girls hide their pregnancies. One colleague of mine did not notice that her overweight daughter who wore big loose shirts on a daily basis was pregnant until she was past five months. Some girls deny their pregnancies; others are afraid to tell. Be sure to tell your daughter that if she ever suspects even a tiny bit that she is pregnant that you hope she will come to you right away. If you do find out that your daughter is in her second or third trimester of pregnancy, seek medical help for her immediately. There are only a limited number of abortion procedures available to her in the later part of the second trimester, and they are expensive and risky. The National Abortion Federation hotline can help. If she decides to continue the pregnancy, she needs prenatal care as soon as possible. Contact a local obstetrician or health department clinic.

"Dad, I Think I'm Gay"

If the possibility of pregnancy strikes fear in many parents' hearts, a teen child announcing that he or she is homosexual or bisexual may evoke similar emotions: surprise, disappointment, fear, guilt. Some parents react with horror and reject their child. In one focus group, young people reported these incidents of bone-chilling rejection.

"They wouldn't talk to me for eight months."

"They said I was dead in their eyes...they took my pictures down."

"My parents burned all my clothes."

Other parents are surprised but not rejecting.

"It's taken them a while to get used to this, but they are coming around."

"My mom cried a lot at first, but she's better now."

Still, some parents respond positively to their teen coming out.

"My mom accepts me and everyone I've been with...she's always been there for me."

"She tells me about things in the gay community. She brings home books by lesbian authors."

Many parents have told me that one of the first things they thought when their children disclosed to them was, "Couldn't be, she or he is just going through a phase." One colleague of mine whose college son came home and announced he was gay said to me over lunch, "He's so young. How could he possibly know yet?"

Remember that accepting one's sexual orientation is part of the developmental task of forming a sexual identity. According to the American Psychological Association, sexual orientation is "an enduring emotional, romantic, sexual, or affectional attraction to another person . . . sexual orientation exists along a continuum that ranges from exclusive homosexuality to exclusive heterosexuality and includes various forms of bisexuality."

Many gay and lesbian adults report that they had an early sense of being different from their peers. About 20 percent recognized that they were gay prior to puberty or just around the time of puberty. Forty percent understood that they were gay in high school, and the other 40 percent self-identified in college. Some studies suggest that young people today are coming out sooner. In one recent study, the average age of self-labeling as gay was 14, with most becoming aware of their attractions between 11 and 16.

By the time a child comes out to a parent, they have probably had these feelings for many years. In general, there was a three-and-a-half-year spread between feeling sexually attracted to someone of the same sex and labeling oneself as gay or lesbian. In one study of gay late adolescents, 25 percent reported first same-gender sexual behavior in childhood, 20 percent in early adolescence, 33 percent in high school, and 10 percent postgraduation. (The remainder had not yet had any sexual experience.) Most of the time the sex was with a best friend or buddy, although one in four had their first sex with a stranger.

Some teens tell their parents that they are bisexual. Some

may indeed have a bisexual orientation: They are attracted to and can fall in love with both men and women. But you should know that as many as two-thirds of gay teens identify themselves as bisexual on the way to self-identification as gay. Your child may indeed be bisexual; they may be confused about their sexual orientation; or they may say that they are bisexual instead of gay to check out your reaction.

Other parents wonder to themselves, "What did I do wrong?" Outdated and incorrect theories used to blame a child's homosexuality on their upbringing. You did not do anything wrong. Sexual orientation is not a choice. People do not choose whether to be gay or straight. There are numerous theories about what causes a person's sexual orientation. According to the American Psychological Association (APA), "Most scientists today agree that sexual orientation is most likely the result of a complex interaction of environmental, cognitive, and biological factors...there is also considerable recent evidence that biology, including genetic or inborn hormonal factors, plays a significant role."

Some parents jump to the conclusion that they can "fix" their gay or lesbian child if they get them to therapy. Therapy cannot change one's sexual orientation. Again, according to the APA, "Homosexuality is not an illness. It does not require treatment and is not changeable." The APA also takes a strong position against "conversion therapies": They believe that such therapy can be harmful, and their official policy states that "any person who enters therapy to deal with issues of sexual orientation has a right to expect that such therapy would take place in a professionally neutral environment absent of any social bias."

That's not to say that your child might not benefit from having help dealing with coming out. Psychological counseling and/or family counseling may be helpful for you and your child. In fact, if you are having trouble dealing with your child being gay, you may wish to deal with *your* issues in therapy. Parents, Friends, and Families of Lesbians and Gays (PFLAG) has excellent materials for parents who have just learned about their child's homosexuality. See the Appendix for their address and the names and addresses of other organizations that deal with gay and lesbian youth and their families.

So what do you do when your child tells you that he or she is gay? Well, the most important thing you can do is *listen*. Find out what they are really telling you. Ask them to tell you more about their feelings and what they are thinking about their sexual orientation. Some teens may be asking for help in dealing with their confusion about their sexual orientation; others may be telling you something that they have known for a long time. And the other important thing you can do right away: *Love your child*. This is the same teenage child he or she was five minutes before they told you. Tell her you love her. Tell him you will support him. Ask how you can help. Look for a local community center that deals with gay and lesbian youth. Make sure that your gay or lesbian teen can meet adults who are gay and lesbian and who lead successful, fulfilling, and healthy lives.

You need to know that it is tough to be a gay teenager, despite greater societal openness about homosexuality. Gay teens face many problems compared to their heterosexual peers. They are five times more likely to be the targets of violence and harassment, three times more likely to be injured in a fight severely enough to warrant medical treatment, and nearly twice as likely to be threatened or injured by someone with a weapon. Gay teens are two times more likely to use alcohol, three times more likely to use marijuana, and eight times more likely to use cocaine and crack than straight teens. Gay and bisexual teens are (depending on the study) three to seven times more likely to attempt suicide than their heterosexual peers. Many report dismay over their same sex attractions, social and emotional isolation, and low self-esteem and abuse not only from peers but also from family members.

But, many do not. Here's what one teen wrote:

"I am part of a new generation of lesbians, gay men, and bisexuals. We come out in college, high school, and even junior high. We're savvy and assertive. We know who we are, and even if we're not sure, we know our options. We know we're not sick. We know we're not the only one. We don't worry about going to hell."

One professional cautions against seeing all gay teens as troubled:

"Viewing all sexual minority youths as overwhelmed or defeated with problems in living diminishes the reality that such individuals are a minority of gay youth. Indeed, many youth with same-sex attractions have unique skills that allow them to cope and even thrive in a culture that seldom recognizes them."

One parent said to me, "Well, at least I don't have to worry about her getting pregnant." Not so . . . most gay and lesbian teens also have heterosexual sexual intercourse. More than 50 percent of gay teen males have had heterosexual intercourse, and more than eight in ten lesbian teen women have. In one study, bisexual and lesbian teen women were just as likely to have had penile-vaginal intercourse, but *more* likely to get pregnant than their straight peers. In fact, bisexual and lesbian women were much more likely to have frequent heterosexual intercourse. Some young lesbians have sex to try to "cure" themselves; others become pregnant to prove to their classmates that they aren't lesbian.

Violence against lesbian and gay teens is common, and takes many forms. Over 90 percent of sexual minority youth report that they sometimes or frequently hear homophobic remarks in their school; one-third of them have heard teachers or other school staff make these comments. More than four in ten say that they have been sexually harassed, one in four say they have experienced physical harassment such as being shoved or pushed, and 13 percent have been physically assaulted. In another study, more than half of out teens reported that they have been subject to physical violence, and more than 90 percent have experienced verbal assaults. As a result, nearly two out of five sexual minority youth say they do not feel safe in school because they are gay, lesbian, bisexual, or transgender.

More and more schools are developing programs to reduce violence and harassment and to increase acceptance of gay and lesbian students. The Los Angeles school system has had a program called Project Ten for gay, lesbian, and bisexual youth since the 1980s. There are more than one thousand schools that have gay-straight student clubs. The Massachusetts Board of Education added sexual orientation to the state's education code. It provides all teachers with training on homophobia and recommends that each high school have a Gay-Straight Alliance. Wisconsin, Connecticut, and California also have laws to protect gay, lesbian, bisexual, and transgender youth. There are national organizations like the National Youth Advocacy Coalition; the Gay, Lesbian, and Straight Education Network; and Parents, Families, and

Friends of Lesbians and Gays devoted to the needs of sexual minority youth. In diverse communities from Boston, Massachusetts; to Houston, Texas; to Kansas City, Missouri; there are local organizations that reach out to gay, lesbian, bisexual, and transgender young people.

Your gay teen needs your support if they are being harassed at school. You need to talk to your teen and let them know that they have rights if they are being harassed. In 1996, a Wisconsin school district had to pay nearly one million dollars to a gay young man named Jamie Nabozny for failing to protect him from orientation-based harassment. Ten mainstream education and mental health groups, including the American Association of School Administrators, the American School Health Association, and the American Academy of Pediatrics, have written a booklet titled "Just the Facts" and distributed one to every school superintendent in the country. The message: "Good schools change the conditions that cause pain for LGBT students—they don't try to change the students themselves." Parents have the right to demand that schools have a zero-tolerance policy for sexual harassment, including harassment because of sexual orientation.

If your child is being harassed at school, you may want to get a copy of "Stopping Anti-gay Abuse of Students in Public Schools" by the Lambda Legal Defense and Education Fund, 120 Wall Street, Suite 1500, New York, NY, 10005, 212-809-8585. They suggest that you report the abuse to the school principal, and not just to guidance counselors or teachers, who may not have an obligation to act. You must document the abuse in writing and get statements from witnesses if you can. If the principal does not resolve the situation, you must be prepared to go to the school superintendent and look into complaint procedures. It is not acceptable for the harassers just to be spoken to. According to Lambda, "Parent conferences combined with detention, suspension, or sometimes expulsion are probably more appropriate. Expulsion is likely the last step in a progressing series of disciplinary measures. It is inappropriate for the school to change the class schedule or seating assignment of the abused student, as if she or he, instead of the misbehaving student, is the problem." If you think you will need to file a lawsuit, Lambda can help.

Leaving High School

The summer between high school and college, or before full-time adult employment, can be a very difficult time for parents. Your child is ready to be an adult. They seem to want to come and go as they please. They come in at all hours of the night. One friend of mine said, "I feel like I'm running a hotel." I think I remember my own mother saying something similar.

Try to negotiate new limits with your older teen. What is acceptable for going out, curfews, sex? Keep talking to them about your values. Allow them greater independence, but remember that they still need your help and still want your love.

Many teens are worried during these last months at home about what is going to happen when they leave their high school boyfriend or girlfriend. If they have been delaying sexual intercourse, some will decide that this is now the time. Some may be more likely to take risks with contraception in order to prove their love. Many will be going away to separate schools, or one may be leaving and the other staying home. Encourage your child to talk with you about these feelings. Let them know that there isn't one right or wrong decision. Encourage them to be honest with their partner about their expectations about exclusivity.

Special Issue

Helping Your Teen Avoid Date Rape and Violence

Nearly one in ten teens, both boys and girls, report being hit, slapped, or physically hurt on purpose by their boyfriend or girlfriend. Many teens and college age women have been the victims of date rape. Sexual violence can take place with people they hardly know, such as on a first date or at a party, but it is also surprising how many young people experience violence in an ongoing relationship. In one study of a thousand high school students, over 45 percent of females and over 43 percent of males reported being the recipient of violence from dating partners at least once. And almost none of these teens tell their parents about this type of violence. They do not tell because they believe that they are some how responsible for the violence; they think that this type of behavior is normal, or they are afraid that parents won't approve of the relationship. (That last one is probably true; I think I would want to kill any boy who laid a hand on Alyssa.) We need to be talking to our teens about dating violence and about date rape. They need to know that they can come to us and that we will help them deal with both kinds of situations.

Teenagers (just like adults) need to understand that violence in a romantic relationship is unacceptable. Both boys and girls should know that they do not have to accept physical and sexual violence in the context of a relationship. Your teen should know that if a dating partner hits them, pushes them, throws objects at them, or displays any violent outburst, they are not at fault and they should get out of the relationship. A teen should know that a person who constantly puts them down in front of others is also being abusive, as well as a partner who tries to control all of their friendships and free time. If you observe any of these behaviors in your teen's relationship, talk to them about it in an undemanding way. Tell them what you see and ask them how they feel about it. Remind them that they are worthwhile and that good relationships are based on respect and caring for the other. Talk to them about whether the relationship should continue. If there is physical violence, do not be afraid to get help. Teenagers can be stalked just like adults, and the violence can escalate. Do not hesitate to call the police or a local domestic violence program for assistance.

Sexual violence at parties is also not uncommon. Talk to your teen about keeping their eyes open if someone makes them feel uncomfortable by staring down at them or by grabbing or pushing them out of the way. Tell them it is better to be rude and take care of themselves than to go with someone who makes them feel uncomfortable. Encourage them to go to parties with a buddy and agree that they will look out for each other. Make sure that they understand that if they leave the party, they tell that buddy where they are going and whom they are going with. Help them understand that they will be less likely to make good decisions after they have been drinking or doing drugs.

Date rape or acquaintance rape is more common than one might think, although there are no national statistics available. In one study, one in six girls report that a date had forced a sexual act on them. One Ivy League college campus reports that they treat an average of sixteen women per weekend evening for date rape. Many teens do not really understand that in today's world, "no" really has to mean "no"; otherwise they may be accused and convicted of rape. For example, in one study, almost two-thirds of students said that it is not rape if the girl dresses provocatively on a date, and one in four said it is not rape if a boy gets his date drunk and she has sex with him after she has already said no to intercourse.

It was not until the mid-1970s that the term "date rape" was coined. I grew up knowing that this "just happened" to women, especially if they had led the boy on. When friends of mine were date raped in college, they did not tell anyone and often worried about what they had done to cause the assault. Today, a teen girl would probably know that she had the legal right to sue her assailant.

There are definite gender differences in how men and women understand forced sexual behavior. In a study of adults, 22 percent of women say they have been forced to have sexual behavior against their will, yet less than 3 percent of men say they have ever forced a woman sexually. Has this 3 percent been really busy? Obviously no. This statistic demonstrates that many more women perceived that they have been forced to have sex while men think they are "just going for it." Communication becomes essential. Teen women and teen men need to learn how to communicate "no" more clearly, and they need to learn how to assure that all sexual behavior is consensual.

Here are some suggestions for teen women, adapted from the "Adolescent Sexual Assault and Harassment Prevention Curriculum":

- Be assertive. Communicate any discomfort you may feel about another person's behavior.

- Avoid the use of alcohol and drugs. Do not get drunk so that you can't handle your own behavior or help a friend that needs you.
- Always have a way home. Have a deal with your parents that they will come get you—no questions asked—if you feel in danger.
- Trust your feelings. If you are feeling pressured, you are. If you are feeling in danger, you may be. Get out of the situation fast.
- Learn to say no to sex and to set sexual limits. Learn how to say yes when you are comfortable with the person and the situation and want to share sexual behaviors.

Here are some suggestions for young men from the American College Health Association:

- Know your sexual desires and limits. Communicate them clearly.
- Accept the woman's decision. No always means no.
- Don't assume a woman wants sex just because of how she dresses or behaves.
- Previous permission for sexual behaviors does not give you permission for the current situation.
- Avoid the use of alcohol and drugs.

Antioch College in Yellow Springs, Ohio, developed an interesting policy on sexual consent for its students. It asks people to ask themselves this basic question: "Why would you want to have a sexual behavior with someone who doesn't like what you are doing?" It teaches students that "If you want to impose your sexual will on someone, your behavior has more to do with dominating the person than with enjoying sexuality and an intimate relationship." It reminds them that getting explicit sexual consent for sex is the only way to avoid charges of rape, which could lead to jail and expulsion. Having a discussion with your teenager about these types of questions could save both of you a lot of trouble later on.

Values Exercise for Chapter Six

Your 19-year-old daughter is coming home for spring break. She tells you on the phone that she is seriously involved with someone and asks if she can bring him home for vacation. You say, "sure," and then she says, "I expect that we can share a room." You say:

- a) "Of course, dear, you can have my room after I kill myself."
- b) "No way, this is still our house and we make the rules."
- c) "Let's talk about this when you get home."
- d) "No problem. We are comfortable with your sexual decisions."

Your 20-year-old son has been dating a woman for three months. You hardly know his new girlfriend. At breakfast, he announces that he is going to get married this summer. You:

- a) Congratulate him!
- b) Ask him if she is pregnant.
- c) Say, "Don't you think this is a little soon, dear?"
- d) Say, "I'd like to hear more about how you know you want to marry her."

Your daughter calls to tell you that she is moving out of the dorm to move in with her boyfriend whom you have never met. You:

- a) Tell her if that she does, you will stop paying tuition.
- b) Ask her to come home so you can discuss this as a family.
- c) Say, "Congratulations! If you're happy, we're happy."
- d) Drive to her college that night so you can talk about this in person.

Chapter 6
Beyond High School
Teens Ages 18–21

Your Almost Adult Child

Your 18- to 21-year-old is almost an adult. They have entered the stage called "late adolescence." They are moving toward adult roles and responsibilities. Many will go away to college; others will start full-time jobs and families. Many late adolescents will achieve the ability to think abstractly, and they will become more aware of their own limitations and how their past will affect their future.

The late adolescent has completed their physical maturation. They have reached their adult height, and their breasts or their penis are at their adult size and shape. Their sexual orientation is likely to be secure: Only 5 percent of college students say that they are unsure about their sexual orientation. Their gender-role definition is also likely to be much clearer, and people who are transgender are increasingly likely to come out at this stage.

Their relationships are changing. They have a greater ability to be empathetic and to enter into mature love relationships.

For many, sexuality becomes more tied to commitment and planning for the future. Six percent of college students ages 18 to 24 are married.

Late adolescents are able to have a more mature relationship with you, their parents, as well. Many parents tell me that they "get their children back" in late adolescence. Because their friends are a little less important at this stage, they can once again feel comfortable spending time with you.

I am not saying that post-high-school teens do not have any problems. They still need parents. Late adolescents face many of the same issues discussed in the chapters on high school; some become even more prominent during the college years. For example:

- One-third of college students are heavy drinkers, and one half of young men and one-third of young women report regular bouts of binge drinking.
- Ten percent of college students have seriously considered committing suicide in the past twelve months.
- Six percent of college-age women say that they have been forced to have sexual intercourse while at college.
- One in four college-age women is thought to have an eating disorder.

The sexual health needs of young adults are intense. More than 85 percent of students in college have had sexual intercourse, and most of them are currently sexually active. Although almost eight in ten report they or their partner used contraception the last time they had intercourse, fewer than one-third of college students report regular and consistent condom use. The result is that young adults ages 18 to 24 have the highest rates of sexually transmitted diseases of any age group, and more than one in five teen women ages 18 and 19 become pregnant each year. Women ages 18 to 24 have one-third of the abortions in the United States. (If you have skipped ahead to this chapter and have a college-age daughter who is facing an unplanned pregnancy, you may want to read the section "Mom, I Think I'm Pregnant" in Chapter Five.)

Preparing Your Child (and Yourself) for College

Over seven million students ages 18 to 24 are enrolled in the nation's 3,600 colleges and universities. One-fourth of all young people this age are currently either full-time or part-time college students.

Most of the books on preparing your child for college talk about issues such as money, what to pack, what to expect from the college, how to stay in touch, and school vacations. I have not seen any that discuss addressing sexuality issues with your child before they leave your home and go off on their own.

As you will read in greater depth below, most college students are involved in sexual relationships. For many young adults, college will be the first time they are completely on their own and responsible for all of their day-to-day decisions, including their decisions about sex, alcohol, and drugs.

This is an emotional time for parents. To be honest, I dreaded the day that we dropped Alyssa off at college. It was going to be incredibly quiet around here without her. I was going to miss her presence and her company. I hoped I would be ready; I knew she would be.

One of my good friends tells the story of dropping her daughter Lindsay off at college. She and her daughter had driven Lindsay's car to the school; her husband and sons flew in to say good-bye. After they left her in her dorm room, they returned to the airport to fly home. She says that when they boarded the plane to return home, they were all crying so hard that the flight attendant offered her condolences on their recent loss of a loved one. And, indeed, it partially felt like that.

It can also be a little bit scary and disconcerting to have your child leave your home. You will no longer be able to set the ground rules for your child's behavior. You won't know what they are doing on a daily or even weekly basis (although e-mail and texting can help a lot!). When you try to reach your child by cell phone, it may be an answering machine. You know that they will be facing important decisions that could affect them for years to come.

It is important that you and your college-bound child talk a lot the summer before they leave, and that you share your hopes and expectations for their time away at school. Don't miss any opportunity for quality time together. Helping them pack for college can be quality time. One mom told me that she said to her daughter, "Humor me by letting me fold your clothes and pack them into suitcases. I know you're going to give up ironing the minute you hit that dorm room." Packing gave them a chance to have hours together in her bedroom that final day before leaving for school.

Susan and Chuck attended one of my workshops for parents on how to handle sexuality issues with children and teenagers. At the end of the workshop, Susan raised her hand. "I agree with what you are saying about giving your values to your younger children, but my daughter is leaving for university. Should we really still be telling her what we want her to do? Isn't it time to let her make her own mistakes?"

"Good question," I answered. Is this the time to stop sharing your values with your child? Is there a time when you will

not want to tell your child what you think? By now, you probably know that I think the answer to that question is "NO!"
Your late adolescent child still needs and indeed wants to hear
your feelings and your values. But, this is also the time to trust
that you have raised your child well. You need to have confidence in the investment you have made in parenting during
the first 18 years.

Of course, we need to let our children make age-appropri-
ate decisions. A 3-year-old child can be given the opportunity
to choose between the red shirt and the blue shirt; that's a 3-
year-old decision. A 6-year-old child can choose what he wants
in his lunch box and if he'd rather take karate or art lessons
after school. A 12-year-old child will be making decisions
about her friends and weekend activities.

Your late adolescent has many important decisions to
make. Late adolescents are faced with increasingly difficult
adult decisions: whether and where to go to college, where to
live, how to support or help support themselves, etc. By now,
your late adolescent has, I hope, learned the steps to good decision making: Identify the options, weigh the consequences,
consult with trusted others, compare the alternatives, anticipate possible outcomes, and make a choice. We need to let
them own these decisions. The message you ultimately want to
communicate to your late adolescent is, "I trust your ability to
make a good decision and to use your good judgment."

But, and this is a big but, they still want to hear from you.
You are still their parents. They still look to you for guidance,
input, and your values. You are the only people who can give
them your values; no one else cares the same way you do about
their well-being. In one study, more than half of college students enrolled in a health education class said that it was very
important to them to talk with their parents about health

issues, and they ranked sex, drugs, alcohol, and HIV/AIDS as the most important subjects for discussion.

So, talk to them. Listen to them. Ask them questions. Listen some more. Remember what teenagers really need is a good listening to. Share your hopes and dreams for them, but acknowledge to them that they have the right to choose a different path. Make sure they know that there is not just one right path. Tell them that you love them and you will always be there for them, even as they get older. Tell them that you expect that they will make mistakes and that you are there if they ever get into trouble. Ask them what you can do to help them make the transition to college easier. Listen again.

Many of the subjects I have discussed in early chapters can be brought up again. Remind your child about your family values about sexual relationships. Make sure that they are knowledgeable about contraception, condoms, and safe sex. Be sure they know the warning signs of the most common sexually transmitted diseases. Review the information about sexual violence and date rape prevention. Talk about what is involved in a healthy relationship.

Before your daughter leaves for college, I think it is a good idea to set up an appointment for her with a gynecologist or family planning clinic. Generally, physicians recommend that a teen woman have her first pelvic exam and PAP smear at around age 18, whether or not she is sexually active. She will have an opportunity to talk with a health care professional about her questions about sexuality and arrange for contraception if it is needed. Similarly, I think it is a good idea for your son to have a physical examination before he leaves for school. Be sure the provider has experience with adolescents and young adults and is able to offer sexually transmitted disease screening on site. (By the way, this is also the time if your child hasn't had one, to make sure he or she is immunized against Hepatitis B, one of the most preventable sexually transmitted diseases, and HPV, a cause of cervical cancer.)

The reality that your late adolescent is most likely going to be involved in a sexual relationship while they are away at school makes these discussions even more important.

The Late Adolescent Who Lives at Home

Not all teenagers attend college, and some who do will also continue to live at home. The important thing to remember is that your late adolescent is almost an adult, and that you will need to renegotiate parts of your relationship.

Few of these areas have anything to do with sexuality. You will want to discuss issues such as: Does your now-working child contribute to the rent? Which household responsibilities do they need to assume? Who will do their cooking and laundry? What about curfews? Alcohol use in your home?

There are some sexuality issues that may arise at this stage. If your 19- or 20-year-old continues to live in your home, you may want to discuss:

- Can they entertain their adult friends at your home?
- Can they entertain when you aren't home?
- Can they entertain in their bedroom?
- Do they continue to have a curfew?
- Do they need to call you if they are going to be late?
- Is it acceptable for them to spend the night away from home? Do they need to call you to let you know?
- Can they have a lover spend the night in your house? In their room?
- Is their room completely private or can you go in there?

You need to think through how much you really want to know about your late adolescent's personal life. Some parents want to know everything and hope that their child will be completely open with them about their relationships. Others really do prefer a "don't ask, don't tell" policy. Remember, you don't want to ask questions that you really don't want to know the answer to!

In many ways, you need to think about your almost adult child as a "roommate" rather than a child under your control. You would offer a roommate advice and council if they were getting involved in a situation that you thought was unwise, but you wouldn't "lay down the law" about their behavior. Respect, open communication, and negotiation are the hallmarks of a good "roommate arrangement"—and a parent/late-adolescent relationship.

This time after high school may be a difficult transition—for both of you. It may be hard to resist saying, "As long as you are in our house, you will obey our rules." But try. Your relationship will be better for it. (And if you really can't find a way to live together as adults, it is time to start helping your late teen develop a plan to live on their own.)

Sexual Behavior: What to Expect

Well, the simple answer is "sex." By the time they are 19, 77 percent of girls and 85 percent of boys have had penile-vaginal sexual intercourse. Sexual activity for late-adolescent dating couples is the norm. Most gay, lesbian, and bisexual young adults will have had their first sexual experiences with someone of the same gender, if they haven't before.

There has not been a well-done national survey of sexual practices of all young people ages 18 to 21, but there was a 1995 government-funded study of college students that included questions about sexual behaviors. We do know that there has been a considerable change in sexual mores on college campuses during the past forty years. Before the late 1960s when some of my readers went to college, there were strict rules on campuses about men and women socializing. Older readers may remember the "one foot on the floor" rule: Women were allowed to have men in their dorm room only if the door was open and each had one foot on the floor. Curfews were common. Coed dorms were non-existent.

Well, we baby boomers helped change all that. Remember as you struggle with your new college student's freedom that it was our generation that insisted on being treated as adults when we were away at school. Coed dorms are now the rule; it is now curfews that are non-existent. A recent article in the *New York Times* about my own alma mater talked about a "clothing-optional dorm."

Most studies of college students report that between three-quarters and 90 percent has had sexual intercourse. The percentage of people having multiple sexual partners or casual sex has increased dramatically over the past twenty-five years. More than one-third of college students have had sexual intercourse during their lifetime with six or more partners.

However, one in six college students are virgins, and they need special support. I remember thinking that I was the only freshman at Wesleyan University who was a virgin. I felt tremendous pressure thirty years ago to have intercourse; no doubt, these virgin college students feel as much or more pressure today. In one recent study of college virgins, the young people reported that they were both proud and anxious about their virginity status. Most of the virgins reported that they had not yet had intercourse because they had not met the right person or because they hadn't yet been in love or in a relationship long enough to have sex. Fears about pregnancy, STDs, and AIDS were the second, third, and fourth most important reasons. Many fewer reported that it was their religious beliefs (reason number seven) or that they were not interested in sex (reason number thirteen).

The majority of late adolescents are involved in a steady, monogamous relationship. In several studies, between half to almost three-quarters of undergraduate students said that they were in a monogamous love relationship. More than seven in ten sexually active college students reported only having sex with one partner in the past three months.

However, most young adults are what health professionals label "serially monogamous": That is, they are sexually exclusive with one partner at a time, but change partners over time. Contraceptive use seems to change over the course of these relationships. Condoms are usually used first, both for contraception as well as for disease prevention. Once the relationship is seen as established (often defined by college students as exclusivity for about one month), condoms are often replaced by birth control pills, as the students perceive that they no longer need to protect themselves against sexually transmitted diseases. Condom use is twice as likely in casual relationships than in monogamous relationships.

College students frequently cite monogamy as the reason that they do not use condoms. However, among students who say they are monogamous, almost half had *more* than one sexual partner in the past year. In fact, in one study, students who said they had been in a monogamous relationship in the past year actually had more sexual partners than students who had not been part of such a relationship. In addition, more than one in four college men say that they would lie about their sexual history in order to have sex. Your college-age student needs to understand that short-term serial monogamy is not a safe strategy for the prevention of STDs.

But the good news for most parents is that today's college students are actually more conservative about sex than their older brothers and sisters. Since 1974, a national survey has asked college freshman whether they agree with this statement, "If two people really like each other, it's all right for them to have sex even if they've known each other for a very short time." In 1987, more than half of college freshman agreed with this statement; in 1995, probably because of growing awareness about HIV and AIDS, only 43 percent did.

However, many more young adults are sexual adventurers, as compared to their high school brothers and sisters. Nearly one-third of 18- to 24-year-olds have had six or more sexual partners. In one study, one-third of the men and the women had had vaginal intercourse with more than five partners. In a national phone survey of college students, one-third of the men and one-fifth of the women reported that they had *nine* or more partners. And the study results are pretty consistent; the students with the greatest number of sexual partners are the least likely to use condoms consistently, least likely to talk about safer sex with a potential partner, least likely to discuss the prevention of HIV, and least likely to feel comfortable talking about these issues with a partner when compared to young people who have had only one or two sexual partners. The results are predictable as well: Sexual adventurers have higher levels of sexually transmitted diseases and unintended pregnancies.

The good news is that many of today's late adolescents are protecting themselves. Nearly eight in ten use a contraceptive method to prevent pregnancy. However, only slightly more than one-quarter say they always or almost always use condoms. And, one in five said they almost never did so. As a result, one in five males and nearly one in three 18- to 21-year-olds have been infected with a sexually transmitted disease.

Your young adult needs some basic information about contraception and condoms, but they may need some other information as well. Given the propensity for serial monogamy during these years, they need to know:

- Sexually active older adolescents are at risk for both pregnancy and STDs.
- Latex condoms are the only effective method for both pregnancy and STD prevention.
- Using multiple methods (one for contraception and condoms for STD prevention) makes good sense.
- Condoms also have to be used for fellatio and dental dams for cunnilingus.
- Many people misrepresent their sexual history.
- A monogamous relationship is not always monogamous.
- Many monogamous relationships are short term, and condoms need to be used unless pregnancy is desired.
- Young people who have had more than one sexual partner should be tested regularly for HIV and other sexually transmitted diseases.
- Young women who have had sexual intercourse should have an annual gynecological exam and PAP smear.

But the mechanics of sexuality and safe sex are only one aspect of sharing your values about sexuality with your late adolescents. This is also an important time to be talking about relationships.

Relationships

Your 18- to 21-year-old is probably beginning to have more serious romantic relationships. In one study, more than half of the men and six in ten of the college age women report that they are in an exclusive love relationship. One in six men and one in four women aged 18 to 24 are married, and many more may be cohabitating. In fact, one statistical study found that while young people have postponed the age at which they first marry, they have not postponed the age at which they first set up housekeeping with a romantic partner. In other words, if cohabitating couples are counted as married, the age of first marriage is similar to what it was in 1970.

Although I couldn't find any statistics about cohabitation among late adolescents, overall we know that it has become much more common. Before 1990, cohabitation was actually illegal in all 50 states. I can remember when it was referred to quite seriously as "living in sin." According to the Bureau of the Census, nearly 4.1 million heterosexual couples cohabitate and nearly 1.5 million homosexual couples do so.

Many college-age couples move in together off campus. These relationships are generally not long term; in most cases, they last two years or less. You will need to think through your own values and what you want to communicate to your children if you discover that they are cohabitating on campus. If you disapprove, will you continue to financially support them through college? If you threaten to withdraw financial support, they are much more likely to quit college, and may have fewer employment opportunities—and a greater risk for pregnancy. How will you handle their visits to your home? Do you prefer to adopt the "don't ask, don't tell" philosophy, or do you want to know?

Other 18 to 21 year olds decide that they are ready for marriage. It is probably less common today than it was thirty years ago for women to drop out of college to get married; more couples choose to cohabitate or get married and stay in school.

Your late adolescent at 18 and 19 has a legal right in every state to get married without your consent. But that does not mean that you do not have a role in helping them prepare for marriage or giving your values about marriage at this age.

You may want to help them assess their readiness for marriage. Is your child really ready to share their life with another person? How will getting married now affect their education and employment plans? Are they ready to settle down? Have they thought through the financial realities of marriage? Are they mature enough to make the compromises that marriage entails? Are they ready to separate enough from the family of their childhood (you!) in order to begin to develop this new family?

You may also want to help them assess whether their relationship is likely to be a successful marriage. Research indicates that in marriages that last, the partners are friends who communicate well. They can handle negative emotions, and they have good conflict resolution skills. They trust each other and both are committed to the idea of marriage as a lifelong union. They have shared interests, and they are flexible. They nurture and comfort each other, offering encouragement and support. They understand that love and sex are only two of the important criteria for marriage. There must also be friendship, trust, communication, shared values, shared vision, and commitment.

Whether or not your child is in a cohabitating, married, or dating relationship, they may need your advice on deciding if the relationship is a good one. Here are some criteria from the Go Ask Alice site of Columbia University's Health Education program for a healthy relationship. They say that in a healthy relationship, you:

- Treat each other with respect.
- Feel secure and comfortable.
- Resolve conflicts satisfactorily.
- Enjoy the time you spend together.
- Support one another.
- Take interest in each other's lives.
- Have privacy in the relationship.
- Trust each other.
- Enjoy sex together and are sexual by choice.
- Communicate clearly and openly.
- Have other friends.
- Are honest about your past.
- Know that most people in your life are happy about the relationship.

Supporting your child's romantic relationship can help strengthen it. If you feel your child may be being abused or hurt, refer to the Special Issues section in Chapter Five to find ideas on how to help them. If you wish they would wait until they were finished with school before they make a lifelong relationship decision, be sure to share that as well. But, try to welcome this new person into your home and your family. Get to know him or her before judging them. Think twice about expressing your displeasure about a relationship. Remember, this could be the parent of your grandchild!

"But You Know We Sleep Together"

The one topic that came up, again and again, when I talked with parents of college-age students was the issue of whether their late adolescent could sleep with (and by inference have sexual intercourse with) their dating partner at their parents' home.

Susan and Bob are good friends of mine who work in the sexuality field. Their daughter Ashley is smart, funny, and has a great relationship with her parents. While she was a senior in high school, she was seriously involved with a boyfriend and Susan gave her condoms and helped her get birth control pills. Susan told her daughter that she thought sexual intercourse was not healthy for her or her relationship, but told me, "I knew she was going to make her own decision, and I wanted to be sure she was protected."

During her sophomore year of college spring break, Susan, Bob, and Ashley took a ski trip together. Ashley met Sam and fell in love. She and Sam spent the summer traveling in Europe together and came back to visit Susan and Bob before returning to their respective colleges. And Susan, with a wry smile, said to me, "I made up the guest room in the basement."

Now, surely Susan and Bob knew that by this point, Ashley and Bob were engaging in some type of sexual activity and it probably included intercourse. They knew and trusted their daughter; they knew and liked her boyfriend. It was a relationship that was caring, trusting, and mature.

As we sat in their kitchen, they explained to me, "We're just not comfortable with it. We do have a younger daughter, and we're not ready to talk with her about Ashley's sexual behavior. But it's more than that, it seems like an invasion of our privacy."

This struck a chord with me. My parents divorced when I was in my early twenties. One night, when Ralph and I were visiting my mother shortly after we were married, she told me that she had been seeing someone for some time who was special. She asked if we would be all right with him spending the night when he was visiting. To my amusement, I reacted negatively. I just didn't want to deal with my mother's overt sexuality. I think I may react the same way when Alyssa comes home and asks.

Here are some reasons parents told me that they are comfortable having their son and daughter sleep with someone in their own homes:

- They are nearly adults.
- I know they are having sex.
- I don't want to encourage them to sneak around.
- I appreciate the honesty and caring of their relationship.
- I'd rather know than not know.

Here are some reasons parents told me that they aren't comfortable having their son and daughter sleep with someone in their own homes:

- They aren't married.
- It's against our values.
- I don't want to send the wrong message to their younger brother or sister.
- It makes me uncomfortable.
- I'm concerned that this relationship won't last, and next year they will want to bring home another person.
- I don't want to seem like I'm giving permission.

Where are you? What factors are important to you to consider? Talk to your spouse or partner as well: How will you deal with it if one of you thinks it is all right and the other does not? If you are not comfortable, what will you do if your child decides to stay in a nearby motel or hotel?

Although this may seem like a difficult problem for parents of college-age students, many parents face much more challenging and life-changing issues.

Teens Who Are Transgender

In the last chapter, I talked about how you might respond if your child tells you that he or she thinks they might be gay or lesbian. About 40 percent of gay adults say that they finally resolved their confusion about their sexual orientation during late adolescence. I have spoken to many parents whose teens come home from their first semester at college and announce that they are gay. Often, these young people have known this about themselves for some time; the independence they have gained at college allows them to come out to their parents for the first time. Most of the issues that I discussed in the last chapter are relevant here: If you have just learned your college-age student is gay, lesbian, or bisexual, you may want to reread that section.

But if you think it might be hard to learn that your child is gay or lesbian, imagine the parent who finds out their child is transgender. I find it hard to imagine the shock it would be to find out that my son understood himself to be my daughter or my daughter to be my son. And, yet, this is exactly the situation that some parents of transgender children face.

Let me try to explain. A person who is transgender is, according to PFLAG, "someone whose gender identity or expression differs from conventional expectations of masculinity or femininity. Gender identity is one's internal sense of being male or female, and for most people, there is no conflict between gender identity and their biological sex." People who are transgender know that their biological sex is different than their gender identity. It's important to note that gender identity is not the same as sexual orientation: People who are transgender can be heterosexual, homosexual, or bisexual.

Transgender people include:

- Transsexuals, who feel such intense discomfort with their gender that they seek to change their biological sex.
- Cross-dressers, formerly called transvestites, who express their gender by wearing clothes of the other sex.
- People who identify as third gender, and disregard masculine and feminine labels.
- Intersexuals (formerly called hermaphrodites), who are born with ambiguous genitalia and who have a different gender identity than the one they were assigned at birth.

For the most part, you will probably not know if your child is a cross dresser. Many cross dressers do so in private, never telling their families and friends about it. Most cross dressers do so for sexual gratification and anxiety reduction, and contrary to popular belief, most are heterosexual and will marry. Issues related to cross dressing then become an issue for the married couple.

Parents of children who were born with ambiguous genitalia have obviously been dealing with these issues throughout their child's life. However, some intersexual high school and college students are first beginning to express a gender identity different than the one you and physicians may have assigned them at birth. If this is the case, they are likely to be quite angry with you, and you will both need counseling and support. The Intersex Society of North America may be able to offer help: www.isna.org.

Parents of transsexual children may face the most intense need for support. In an open letter from a transsexual woman named Sheila Mengert to the parents of transsexual children, she says, "What lies ahead for you will require the same courage, effort, commitment, and love that is required when anyone is forced by circumstances to face facts that one would prefer to deny or to ignore."

Just as you do with a child who comes to you with any problem, the first thing to do is *listen*. You may feel many things: shock, confusion, anger, fear, embarrassment, and guilt. You will probably also have concerns about your child's health, safety, employment, education, and future relationships. "What you need to understand is the agony that person went through to tell you," says one transsexual young adult. "The only reason they did it is because they care for you, and they believe you need to know." You also need to understand that, in the words of the PFLAG pamphlet, "The desire to modify the body to conform to one's gender identity cannot be adequately explained by someone who is transsexual, nor can it be fully understood by someone who is not."

Most parents will react to this news by feeling a sense of guilt: "What did I do wrong raising my child?" You need to know that you did not do *anything* to cause your child's gender identity. There is no research to show that parents could prevent this. In fact, although the research is still ongoing, many believe that transsexualism is caused by genetic factors, prenatal hormonal influences, and other chemicals in the brain. Assigning gender at birth to intersexual children was standard practice twenty years ago; remember you did what was considered best when you assigned your child's sex when they were born.

So, what do you need to know now that you know that your child is transgender? You and your child may need help from a professional who is trained in "gender dysphoria." This person can help you and your child make the adjustments needed, especially for transsexuals who will be going through a difficult transition phase. You can find referrals to qualified professionals through the Harry Benjamin International Gender Dysphoria Association (www.hbigda.org) or the International Foundation for Gender Education (www.ifge.org). Many transsexuals choose hormone treatment and surgery, but increasingly, some people are choosing to change their appearance and their presentation of their gender without the surgery.

Here is some of what your transgender child needs, adapted from a terrific website on transgender youth, Mermaids (www.mermaids.freeuk.com):

- Where to go for help, support, and advice;
- Where to meet people who are transgender and have successfully transitioned;
- Help in searching for suitable clothes;
- Advice on changing names and legal documents;
- Advice on dealing with their college or university; and
- Support and encouragement.

Here's advice from one parent of a transsexual, male to female, who transitioned in her teens. This mom writes:

The young transsexual can be a constant source of heartaches and headaches for those who love them—so how do we cope? The essential tools are:

- *A good basic understanding of the problems that they are facing;*
- *Lots of love, an awful lot of patience;*
- *A shoulder to cry on; and*
- *A good sense of humor.*

She goes on to say,

> *So, if you're in a similar situation, find out as much information on the subject as you can. It's worth contacting some of the adult transgender support groups as they can also provide valuable information. Most important, ask your young transsexual how best you can help them. Be patient with them—this problem takes time to sort out. But also ask them to be patient with you. No one can change their identity almost overnight and expect everyone else to keep up with them.*

What does your transgender child need most of all? Like all of our children, they need to know you love them and that you are there for them. Remember, this is still your child, even if you literally feel that you have lost a son and are about to gain a daughter. Or lost a daughter and are about to gain a son. Here's a message one parent left on her transgender child's answering machine, "It doesn't matter to us whether you are Charles or Terri; we love you regardless. We love our daughter as much as we love our son." I hope I would do as well.

Perspective

It can be tough to be a parent of a late adolescent. You need to make the transition from the parent who sets the limits, defines the boundaries, supervises the day-to-day comings and goings, and participates in the decision making to the parent who offers advice, support, and love. As one of my friends told her daughter on the night of her eighteenth birthday, "Honey, I think of myself as off your board of directors. I am also still available to serve on your advisory committee."

But remember, ever since your child's first steps and their

2-year-old tantrums, your child has been getting ready to one day leave you for the world of adulthood. Celebrate this time together! You've made it!

Remember to keep your perspective on what's really important during your child's young adult years. Here is a version of a letter that one college student reportedly sent home:

Dear Mom and Dad:

It's been three months since I left for college. I should have written sooner. I will bring you up to date now. Before you read further, please sit down. I'm not kidding . . . sit down.

I'm getting along pretty well now. The skull fracture and the concussion I got when I jumped out of the window of my dorm room when it caught fire are pretty well healed now. I only spent two weeks in the hospital, and now I can see almost normally and only get those terrible headaches once a day or so.

Fortunately, a gas station attendant down the street saw me jump and called the fire department and the ambulance. He also visited me at the hospital, and since I had nowhere to live, invited me to share his apartment with him. He is a very fine man and we have fallen deeply in love and are planning to get married. We haven't set the exact date yet, but it will be before my pregnancy begins to show.

Yes, Mom and Dad, I am pregnant. I know how much you are looking forward to being grandparents, and I know you will welcome the baby. The reason we had to delay getting married is that my boyfriend has some type of minor infection, which kept us from passing our premarital blood test, and I caught it from him. They told us it would clear up after we finish taking all of the penicillin.

I know you will welcome him into our family with open arms. He is kind, and although he didn't finish high school, he is ambitious. Although he is of a different culture and religion, I know you will love him as I do. At least once he learns enough English.

Now that I have brought you up-to-date, I want to tell you that there was no fire; I do not have a concussion or a skull fracture; I was not in the hospital; I am not pregnant; I am not engaged; I do not have syphilis; and there is no man of any kind in my life.

I am however getting D's in history and biology, and I wanted you to see those marks in their proper perspective.

Your loving daughter

Perspective. Try to remember what's really important; stay involved with your young adult's life; keep talking and keep listening.

Afterword

$\mathbf{B}$efore I had my children, I thought it was a cliché when people said that parenting was one of life's most rewarding experiences. Now I know it is. And helping your children grow up to become sexually healthy adults is one of the joys and responsibilities of good parenting.

I am sometimes asked whether I really think dealing with these issues from the time children are in diapers makes a difference. After all, people say to me, "My parents never talked to me at all about sex, and I'm doing okay." Sometimes, after that statement, they tell me about their troubled relationship, or they ask me their questions about a sexual dysfunction they are experiencing. Sometimes, they tell me stories about how their sense of their sexual selves was hurt during childhood or adolescence through ignorance, fear, or abuse.

It is difficult in American culture to be a sexually healthy adult. I have defined America as "moderately erotophobic." We are relaxed enough about sexuality to have sexual relationships, but too many of us carry within us a dark box of shame, guilt, misinformation, fear, and negative experiences about our sexuality. And that dark box can get in the way of the type of adult relationships we want to have.

I want something different for my children. And, if you have read this far, I believe you do, too.

In this book, and in its predecessor for parents of younger children, *From Diapers to Dating: A Parent's Guide to Raising Sexually Healthy Children*, I have tried to help you lay the foundation for your children to grow up to be sexually healthy adults. If you have followed some of the advice in these books, I hope that you have created a relationship with your children to openly and honestly discuss sexual issues. I hope you have shared your family values on these important issues. I hope you have already seen some of the results of open communication about sexual topics.

Parents of adult children tell me that one of the greatest satisfactions in life is knowing that their adult children are leading happy, productive, and fulfilled lives. Both you and your children deserve to be sexually healthy.

In 1991, the National Guidelines Task Force, a group of twenty leading health, education, and medical professionals, developed a list of the life behaviors of a sexually healthy adult. A sexually healthy adult is not defined by how often one has sex, or even how good the sex you experience is. Remember, sexuality is about who we are, not what we do with a part of our bodies.

Here's a final quiz for you and your adult children to take.
Place a check next to each question you can answer "yes" to.
Do you:

❑ Like your own body?

❑ Have good relationships with both men and women?

❑ Feel comfortable with your sexual orientation?

❑ Treat straight, gay, lesbian, and bisexual people with
equal respect?

❑ Have friends whom you can confide in?

❑ Have good relationships with members of your family?

❑ Feel good about your primary romantic, intimate relationship if you are in one?

❑ Avoid exploiting and manipulating people?

❑ Think about your values on sexuality issues?

❑ Take responsibility for your own behavior?

❑ Generally make good decisions?

❑ Communicate effectively with your family, friends, and
partner?

❑ Express your sexuality in a way congruent with your values?

❑ Understand that you can have and enjoy sexual feelings
without necessarily acting upon them?

❑ Discriminate between sexual behaviors that are life
enhancing and those that might be harmful to yourself
or others?

❑ Express your sexuality while respecting the rights of others?

❑ Seek new information when you need it about your sexuality?

❑ Use contraception (if you are heterosexual and fertile)
all the time?

❑ Use condoms all the time (if you are sexually active in
a non-monogamous relationship or one where you don't

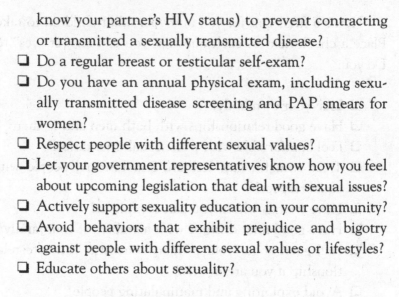

know your partner's HIV status) to prevent contracting
or transmitted a sexually transmitted disease?

❑ Do a regular breast or testicular self-exam?

❑ Do you have an annual physical exam, including sexually transmitted disease screening and PAP smears for
women?

❑ Respect people with different sexual values?

❑ Let your government representatives know how you feel
about upcoming legislation that deal with sexual issues?

❑ Actively support sexuality education in your community?

❑ Avoid behaviors that exhibit prejudice and bigotry
against people with different sexual values or lifestyles?

❑ Educate others about sexuality?

Most of us will not be able to answer "yes" to *all* these
questions, but we can all move in this direction. If you have
been educating your children about sexuality throughout their
lives, it is likely that they will score well on this quiz when they
reach adulthood. What a gift that will be to them and their
future spouse or significant other!

It is also a gift that they are likely to pass on to their children—your grandchildren! When parents talk to their children
about sexuality issues, their children grow up to be parents who
talk to *their* children. And so on. You are helping to create a
future world of sexually healthy adults—where every child
learns that our bodies are wonderful and no child is violated;
where every question receives an honest answer; and where
every preteen and teenager has the information and skills to
make good, healthy decisions about their sexuality. In a world
of sexually healthy adults, all of us would have fulfilling relationships based on honesty, equality, respect, and joy. It is the
world that I hope for my children and my grandchildren.

Appendix
Sources for
More Information

I hope that this book has answered many of your questions and concerns. But parenting an adolescent is challenging, and I expect that you may have many other questions. I believe strongly in seeking out additional information. This appendix includes resources for you and resources for your teen children to turn to for more information. It includes current books for your teens on sexuality. It also includes organizations, websites, and hotlines that might be useful.

My daughter Alyssa helped me research this chapter when she was sixteen. She personally gave a "thumbs up" for the books for teens and the teen websites. I reviewed them as well and visited the sites for parents. Of course, you will need to decide which books and which sites are useful for you. The books and the sites represent a wide range of values about sexuality; look for ones that support your family values. The audiences for the books and websites also range from early adolescents to late adolescence. Websites change quickly; this list is current as of this writing. Of course, these books and sites do not take the place of medical information or counseling; if you need assistance, contact your physician or mental health provider.

BOOKS FOR TEENS

Akagi, Cynthia. *Dear Larissa: Sexuality Education for Girls, Ages 11–17.* Littleton, Colorado: Gylantic Publishing, 1994.

———. Dear Michael: *Sexuality Education for Boys, Ages 11–17.* Littleton, Colorado: Gylantic Publishing, 1996.

Bass, Ellen and Kate Kaufman. *Free Your Mind: The Book for Gay, Lesbian, and Bisexual Youth.* New York: HarperPerennial Library, 1996.

Basso, Michael, *The Underground Guide to Teenage Sexuality,* 2nd ed. Minneapolis: Fairview Press, 2003.

Bell, Ruth, *Changing Bodies, Changing Lives.* New York: Random House, 1998.

Columbia University Health Education Program, *The Go Ask Alice Book of Answers.* New York: Holt, 1998.

Drill, Esther; Heather McDonald; and Rebecca Odes, *Deal with It.* New York: Pocket Books, 1999.

Heron, Ann. *Two Teenagers in Twenty: Writings by Gay and Lesbian Youth.* Los Angeles: Alyson Publications, 1994.

Lieberman, James and Karen Lieberman, *Like It Is: A Teen Sex Guide.* Jefferson, North Carolina: McFarland and Company, 1998.

Weston, Carol. *Girltalk: All the Stuff Your Sister Never Told You,* 4th ed. New York: HarperPerennial Library, 2004.

White, Lee. *The Teenage Human Body Operator's Manual.* Eugene, Oregon: Northwest Media, Inc., 1998.

WEBSITES ON ADOLESCENT SEXUALITY

For Teens

*Responds individually to e-mail queries

www.avert.org
   AVERT: AIDS Education and Research Trust

This site provides a wide variety of information about sexuality, including AIDS, birth control, puberty, how to deal with relationship issues, and resources for gay teens.

www.beinggirl.com
This site for younger teens is primarily about menstruation, but also includes information about relationships and STDs.

* www.goaskalice.columbia.edu
Go Ask Alice!
This site is from the Columbia University Health Education program. Primarily for college students, it offers frank answers and advice on relationships, sexual behaviors, and sexual health.

www.iwannaknow.org
Sponsored by The American Social Health Association
This site specializes in STDs and their prevention; it also includes information on sexuality and a weekly teen chatroom.

www.outproud.org
OutProud: Be Yourself
Outproud is the website of the National Coalition for Gay, Lesbian, Bisexual, and Transgender Youth. The School Resources section is particularly used for issues related to making schools safe places for all youth.

* www.positive.org
Coalition for Positive Sexuality (CPS)
This is a site for teens who are sexually active or thinking about having a sexual relationship. It includes honest information about decision making, contraception, STDs, and pregnancy.

* www.sxetc.org
Sex, Etc.: A Website by Teens for Teens
This site offers frank, honest information on a wide range of sexuality topics, from abstinence to safer sex.

www.teenwire.com
Teenwire
This is the Planned Parenthood Federation of America teen site.

www.youthresource.com
Youth Resource
This is primarily a site for gay, lesbian, bisexual, and transgender youth.

Appendix

For Parents

www.advocatesforyouth.org
Advocates for Youth
Advocates for Youth provides information to professionals and policy makers on adolescent sexual health.

www.aegis.com
AEGIS
This site provides up-to-date medical and social information about HIV/AIDS.

www.cdcnpin.org
CDC National Prevention Information Network
This is the federal government's public information site on sexually transmitted diseases, including HIV/AIDS.

www.teenpregnancy.org
National Campaign to Prevent Teen Pregnancy (NCPTP)
The National Campaign site contains information on teenage pregnancy prevention, including tips for parents.

www.pflag.org
Parents, Family, and Friends of Lesbians and Gays (PFLAG)
PFLAG's site provides very useful and supportive information for parents of GLBT youth, including referrals to local support groups.

www.siecus.org
Sexuality Information and Education Council of the U.S. (SIECUS)
SIECUS's site includes a special forum for parents, including copies of several pamphlets on communicating about sexuality with parents.

www.mediacampaign.org
National Youth Anti-Drug Media Campaign
This site contains information about drug prevention for parents.

226

WEBSITES ON GENERAL ADOLESCENT TOPICS

For Teens

www.bluejeanonline.com
Blue Jean Magazine
Online version of *Blue Jean*, a feminist teen magazine.

www.fda.gov/oc/opacom/kids/html/7teens.htm
On the Teen Scene
The federal government posts information on a variety of health issues, from mono to toxic shock syndrome.

www.gurl.com
GURL.com
This is an edgy, feminist 'zine for teen women.

www.teenvoices.com
Teen Voices Magazine
This is a more mainstream online magazine for teen women, and includes a large link section to other sites.

For Parents

www.adolescenthealth.org
The Society for Adolescent Medicine (SAM)
Although primarily for health professionals, this site provides good information about adolescent health care.

www.ama-assn.org/ama/pub/category/1947.html
American Medical Association
This site, Adolescent Health Online, is written primarily for medical professionals, but it will also help provide parents with general information about adolescent health care.

http://education.Indiana.edu/cas/adol/adol.html
Adolescent Directory On-Line (ADOL)
This site provides good information for parents and professionals on adolescent health and mental health issues.

www.kidshealth.org
KidsHealth
This site includes information for parents on parenting and health issues.

www.search-institute.org
The Search Institute
The Search Institute site includes research on helping build assets in young people and communities.

www.talkingwithkids.org
Talking with Kids about Tough Issues
This site, sponsored by the Kaiser Family Foundation, includes tips for parents on talking about sexuality, HIV/AIDS, violence, alcohol, and drugs.

WEBSITES ON SPECIFIC ISSUES

www.anred.com
Anorexia Nervosa and Related Eating Disorders, Inc. (ANRED)
Information about anorexia, bulima, and binge eating.

www.edap.org
Eating Disorders Awareness and Prevention (EDAP)
Information about preventing eating disorders.

www.edreferral.com
Eating Disorder Referral and Information Center
For referrals for help with eating disorders.

www.glsen.org
Gay, Lesbian, and Straight Education Network (GLSEN)
Help on fighting discrimination against GLBT youth in public schools.

www.gendertalk.com
Gender Talk
Transgender information and referrals.

www.isna.org
Intersex Society of North America (ISNA)
Information for people born with atypical sexual anatomy.

www.rainn.org
Rape, Abuse, and Incest National Network
Help for survivors of rape, sexual abuse, and incest.

NATIONAL TOLL-FREE HOTLINE NUMBERS

AIDS Hotline.. (800) CDC-INFO

Planned Parenthood Federation of America .... (800) 230-7526

National Drug Abuse Hotline .... (800) 662-4357

National Gay and Lesbian Hotline .... (888) 843-4564

National Herpes Hotline .... (800) 227-8922

National Suicide Prevention Hotline.......................... (800) 621-4000

Nutrition and Eating Disorders Hotline .... (800) 366-1655

National Runaways Hotline.. (800) 621-4000

National STD Hotline .... (800) 227-8922

Rape, Abuse, and Incest National Network................ (800) 656-HOPE

References

Advocates for Youth, "Lesbian, Gay, Bisexual, and Transgender Youth: At Risk and Underserved," fact sheet, Washington, D.C., 1998.

Alexander, Christopher, J., "Studying the Experiences of Gay and Lesbian Youth," *Journal of Gay and Lesbian Social Services* (1998), 8:2: 69–72.

American Medical Association adolescent website (www.ama-assn.org/adolhlth).

Armour, Maryellen, "Dating Violence Among Teens," fact sheet, Washington, D.C.: Advocates for Youth, 2000.

American Psychological Association website, "Answers to Your Questions About Sexual Orientation and Homosexuality," (www.apa.org/pubinfo/answers.html).

APA Monitor Online, October 1999, "Court's Sexual Harassment Ruling Puts Schools on Notice," (www.apa.org/monitor/oct99/cf9.html).

Birch, David et. al., "Health Discussions Between College Students and Parents: Results of a Delphi Study." *Journal of American College Health* (1997) 46: 139–143.

Bradsher, Keith, "3 Guilty of Manslaughter in Slipping Drug to Girl," *The New York Times*, March 15, 2000, p. A14.

Brent, David, "Stressful Life Events, Psychopathology, and Adolescent Suicide: A Case Control Study." *Suicide and Life-Threatening Behavior* (1993) 23:3, 179–87.

Brindis, Claire; Susan Pagliaro; and Laura Davis, *Protection as Prevention: Contraception for Sexually Active Teens*. Washington, D.C.: The National Campaign to Prevent Teen Pregnancy, 2000.

Brown, Jane D., "The Media." Unpublished paper prepared for the U.S. Surgeon General's Call to Action, July 1, 2000.

Centers for Disease Control and Prevention, "Youth Risk Surveillance: National College Health Risk Behavior Survey: United States 1995." *Morbidity and Mortality Weekly Report* (November 14, 1997), 46 (ss-6), 1–54.

Centers for Disease Control and Prevention, "Youth Risk Behavior Surveillance—United States, 1997." *Morbidity and Mortality Weekly Report* (August 14, 1998), 47.

Critelli, Joseph and David Suire. "Obstacles to Condom Use: The Combination of Other Forms of Birth Control and Short-Term Monogamy." *Journal of American College Health* (1998) 46: 215–219.

Cyprian, J.; K. McLaughlin; and G. Quint, *Sexual Violence in Teenage Lives: A Prevention Curriculum*. Vermont: Planned Parenthood of Northern New England, 1995.

ERIC Digest, "Latchkey Children." www.ed.gov/databases/ ERIC_Digests/ed290575.

Erikson, Erik H., *Identity: Youth and Crisis*. New York: W. W. Norton and Company, 1968.

Fay, Joe and Jay Yanoff, *What Are Teens Telling Us About Sexual Health?* York, Pennsylvania: York City Bureau of Health, 1999.

Folb, Kate L., "Don't Touch That Dial: TV As A—WHAT?—Positive Influence." *SIECUS Report* (2000), 28:5, 16–18.

Food and Drug Administration, "On the Teen Scene: Good News About Nutrition," revised January 1999.

Funk, Marjorie, *Adolescent Sexual Assault and Harassment Prevention Curriculum*. Florida: Learning Publications, 1995.

Garrison, Karl C., and Karl C. Garrison, Jr., *Psychology of Adolescence*. New Jersey: Prentice Hall, Inc., 1975.

Gay, Lesbian, and Straight Education Network, "GLSEN's National Climate Survey," September 1999, press release.

Greenberg, Jerrold; Clint Bruess; and Debra Haffner, *Exploring the Dimensions of Human Sexuality*. Massachusetts: Jones and Bartlett Publishers, 2000.

Gustavsson, Nora S., and Ann E. MacEachron, "Violence and Lesbian and Gay Youth." *Journal of Gay and Lesbian Social Services* (1998) 8:3: 41–51.

Haag, Pamela, *Voices of a Generation: Teenage Girls on Sex, School, and Self*. Washington, D.C.: AAUW Educational Foundation, 1999.

Haffner, Debra W., editor, *Facing Facts: Sexual Health for America's Adolescents*. New York: SIECUS, 1995.

Hall, G. Stanley, *Adolescence*. New York: Appleton, 1916.

Hatcher, Robert, et.al., *Contraceptive Technology*. New York: Ardent Media, 1998.

Havighurst, Robert, *Developmental Tasks and Education*. Chicago: University of Chicago Press, 1948.

LAMBDA Legal Defense and Education Fund, *Stopping Anti-Gay Abuse of Students in Public Schools*. New York: LAMBDA, 1998.

Kaiser Family Foundation, *Kids and Media @ The New Millenium*. California: Kaiser Family Foundation, November 1999.

Kaiser Family Foundation/ABC Television, *Sex In the 90's*. California: Kaiser Family Foundation, 1998.

Kaiser Family Foundation/Children Now, "Talking With Kids About Tough Issues," *Chart Pack*, 1999.

Kaiser Family Foundation, *Teens Talk About Dating, Intimacy, and Their Sexual Encounters*. California: Kaiser Family Foundation, 1999.

Kann, Laura et. al., "Youth Risk Behavior Surveillance—United States, 1997." *Journal of School Health* (1998) 68:9, 355–369.

Kett, Joseph, *Rites of Passage: Adolescence in America, 1790 to the Present*. New York: Basic Books, 1970.

Lounsbury, John, "Key Characteristics of Middle Level Schools." *ERIC Digest*, 1996.

Magid, Lawrence, "Teen Safety on the Information Highway." On www.safekids.com.

Mengert, Sheila, "An Open Letter to the Parents of Transsexual Children" on www.mermainds.freeuk.com/letter.html.

Meltz, Barbara, "Preteens and the Party Scene." *Boston Globe*, February 10, 2000.

Miller, Kim S. et. al., "Family Communication About Sex: What Are Parents Saying and Are Their Adolescents Listening?" *Family Planning Perspectives*, (1988) 30:5 218–222.

———, "Patterns of Condom Use Among Adolescents: The Impact of Mother-Adolescent Communication." *American Journal of Public Health* (1998) 88:10: 1542–1544.

National Campaign to Prevent Teen Pregnancy, *Peer Potential: Making the Most of How Teens Influence Each Other.* Washington, D.C.: National Campaign to Prevent Teen Pregnancy, 1999.

National Campaign to Prevent Teen Pregnancy, Press release, April 30, 1998.

National Guidelines Task Force, *Guidelines for Comprehensive Sexuality Education, Kindergarten—12th Grade,* 2nd Edition. New York: SIECUS, 1996.

National Research Council and Institute of Medicine, *Risks and Opportunities: Synthesis of Studies on Adolescence.* Michelle D. Kipke, ed., Washington, D.C.: National Academy Press, 1999.

National Vital Statistics Report, October 25, 1999. 47:26.

Neinstein, Lawrence S., *Adolescent Health Care: A Practical Guide.* Baltimore: Urban and Schwarzenberg, 1984.

Nesmith, Andrea; David Burton; and T. J. Cosgrove, "Gay, Lesbian, and Bisexual Youth and Youth Adults: Social Support in Their Own Words." *Journal of Homosexuality* (1999) 37:1: 95–108.

Parents, Families, and Friends of Lesbians and Gays (PFLAG), "Our Trans Children, Second Edition," Washington, D.C.: PFLAG, 1999.

Pleck, J., F. Sonenstein, and L. Ku, "Masculinity Ideology: Its Impact on Adolescent Males' Heterosexual Relationships." *Journal of Social Issues* (1993) 49:3 11–30.

Prince, Alice and Amy Bernard, "Sexual Behaviors and Safer Sex Practices of College Students on a Commuter Campus." *Journal of American College Health* (1998) 47: 11–21.

Public Agenda Online, "Kids These Days." December 1998.

Remafedi, G., "Demography of Sexual Orientation in Adolescents," *Pediatrics* (1992) 89:4: 714–21.

Remafedi, G.; J. Farrow; R. Deisher, "Risk Factors for Attempted Suicides in Gay and Bisexual Youth." *Pediatrics* (1991) 87: 6: 869–875.

Rodriguez, Monica, "SIECUS Forum on Adolescent Sexuality and Popular Culture." *SIECUS Report* (2000) 28:5, 3–5.

Sabo, D., *The Women's Sports Foundation Report: Sports and Teen Pregnancy.* New York: Women's Sports Foundation, 1998.

Saewyc, Elizabeth et. al., "Sexual Intercourse, Abuse, and Pregnancy Among Adolescent Women: Does Sexual Orientation Make a Difference?" *Family Planning Perspectives,* (1999) 31:3, 127–131.

Savin-Williams, Ritch, *And Then I Became Gay.* New York: Routledge, 1998.

Sax, Linda, "Health Trends Among College Freshman." *Journal of American College Health,* (1997) 45: 252–262.

Schindler, Paul, "Sobering New Evidence About Oral Sex," LGNY, 21: 44, February 12, 2000.

Schuster, Mark A.; Robert M. Bell; and David E. Carouse, "The Sexual Practices of Adolescent Virgins: Genital Sexual Activities of High School Students Who Have Never Had Vaginal Intercourse." *American Journal of Public Health* (1996) 86: 11, 1570–1576.

Selverstone, Bob. "Now What Do I Do?" New York: SIECUS, 1996.

Siegel, Judith et. al., "Body Image, Perceived Pubertal Timing, and Adolescent Mental Health." *Journal of Adolescent Health Care* (1999) 25: 155–165.

Simon, Toby and Bethany Golden, *Dating: Peer Education for Reducing Sexual Harassment and Violence Among Secondary Students.* Florida: Learning Publications, Inc., 1966.

Smetana, Judith, "Parenting Styles and Conceptions of Parental Authority During Adolescence." *Child Development* (1995), 66: 299–316.

Sprecher, Susan and Pamela Regan, "College Virgins: How Men and Women Perceive Their Sexual Status." *Journal of Sex Research* 1996) 33:x, 3–15.

Terry, Elizabeth and Jennifer Manlove, *Trends in Sexual Activity and Contraceptive Use Among Teens.* Washington, D.C.: The National Campaign to Prevent Teen Pregnancy, 2000.

Thornton, A. and D. Camburn, "The Influence of the Family on Premarital Sexual Attitudes and Behavior." *Demography* 24:323, 1987.

U. S. Census, www.census.gov/population/socdemo/ms-la/tabms-2.txt.

U. S. Department of Education. "Sexual Harassment: It's Not Academic." Pamphlet, at www.ed.gov/offices/OCR/ocrshpam.html.

Index

About
the Author

Debra W. Haffner, M.Div., M.P.H, has been a parenting educator for more than twenty-five years and has provided presentations to thousands of parent and professional groups, including the National School Boards Association, the U.S. Centers for Disease Control and Prevention, the American Medical Association, the American Psychological Association, and public and private schools throughout the U.S. She speaks regularly about parenting issues, and is a contributor to *The Huffington Post*, has written for WebMD, iVillage, and DrSpock.com, and has been featured on *Oprah*, *The View*, *Today*, and in *Time*, *Newsweek*, *USA Today*, and *U.S. News & World Report*.

She is the author of six books, including *From Diapers to Dating: A Parent's Guide to Raising Sexually Healthy Children*, *Beyond the Big Talk: A Parent's Guide to Raising Sexually Healthy Teens*, and *What Every 21st-Century Parent Needs to Know: Facing Today's Challenges with Wisdom and Heart*.

The recipient of the Distinguished Alumni Award from the Department of Epidemiology and Public Health, Yale University School of Medicine, in 2000, Haffner holds a master's in public health from the Yale University School of Medicine and a master of divinity from Union Theological Seminary. Currently the director of the Religious Institute, she is also an ordained minister with the Unitarian Church in Westport, Connecticut. She previously served for twelve years as president and CEO of SIECUS, the Sexuality Information and Education Council of the United States.

She and her husband are the parents of two children, an adult daughter and a teenage son.

CPSIA information can be obtained
at www.ICGtesting.com
Printed in the USA
JSHW080021310123
37085JS00008B/120